Siddhart

11+
Non-verbal Reasoning

Non-verbal Reasoning Technique

WORKBOOK 1

Dr Stephen C Curran
with Andrea Richardson
Edited by Nell Bond

This book belongs to

Accelerated Education Publications Ltd

Contents

Pages

1. Elements

1.	Shapes	3-7
2.	Fills	8-11
3.	Lines	12-15
4.	Key Questions used in Non-verbal Reasoning	16-19

2. Movements

1.	Reflection	20-22
2.	Rotation	23-25
3.	Superimposition	26-28
4.	Transposition	29-31

3. Manipulations

1.	Size	32-34
2.	Addition	35-37
3.	Subtraction	38-40
4.	Frequency (Counting)	41-43

4. Patterns

1.	Repetition	44-46
2.	Cumulation	47-49

5. Layering

1.	Level One	50-52
2.	Level Two	53-55

© 2011 Stephen Curran

Chapter One
ELEMENTS

Non-verbal Reasoning questions combine three **Elements**:
Shapes • Fills • Lines

1. Shapes
a. Standard Palette

This comprises all 'closed' geometrically defined shapes.
Triangles • Quadrilaterals • Polygons • Circles

(i) Triangles

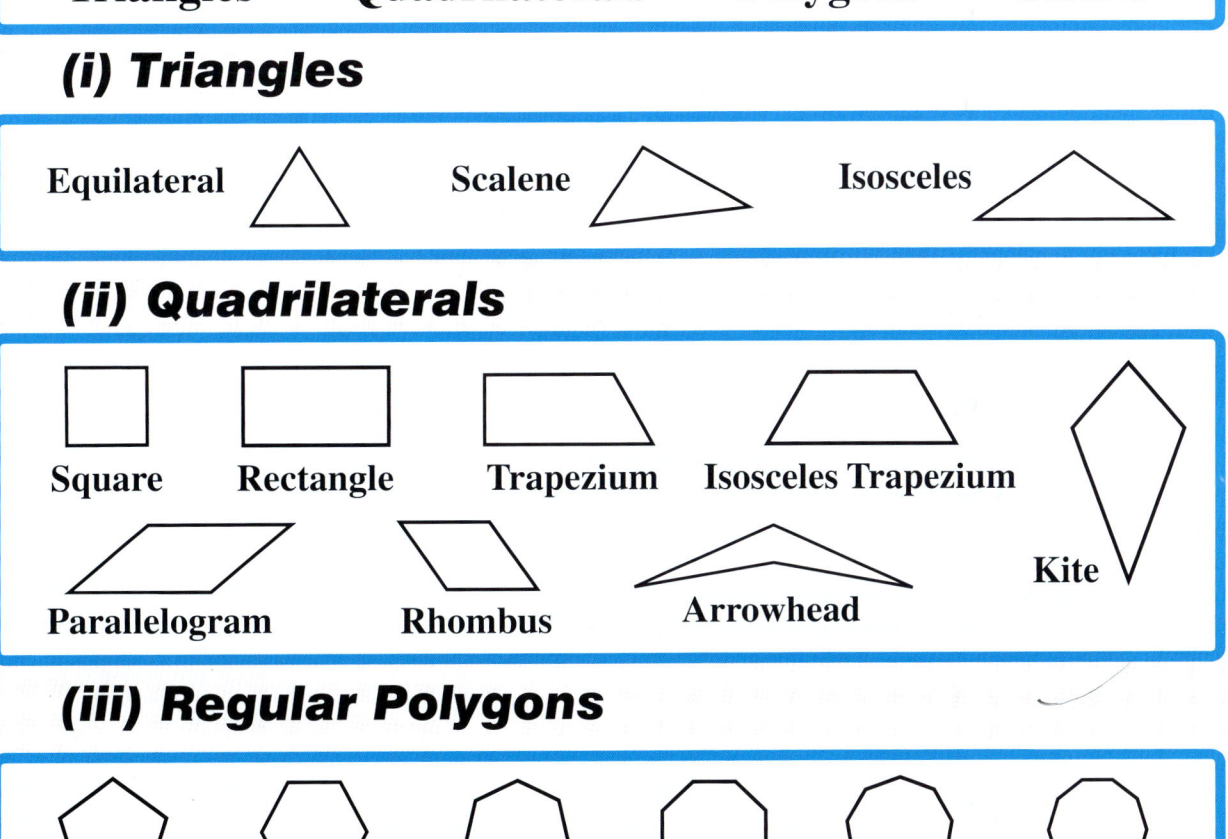

(ii) Quadrilaterals

(iii) Regular Polygons

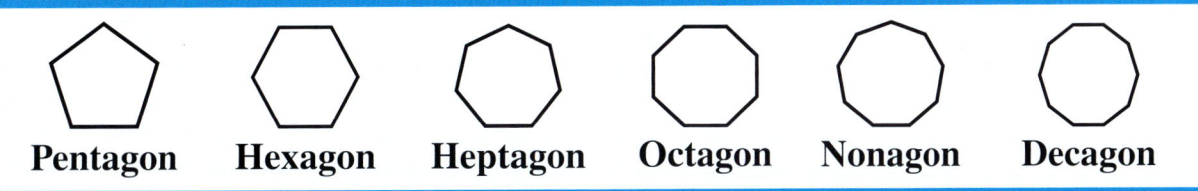

(iv) Circular Shapes

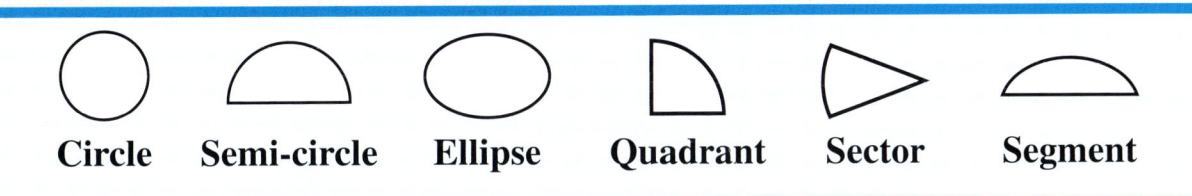

(v) Irregular Polygons

Irregular shapes have unequal sides and angles.

General Quadrilateral   Pentagon   Hexagon

b. Specialist Palette

This comprises everyday recognisable 'closed' shapes.

Straight-edged Shapes • Curved Shapes

Other shapes could be shown that are not in these palettes.

(i) Straight-edged Shapes

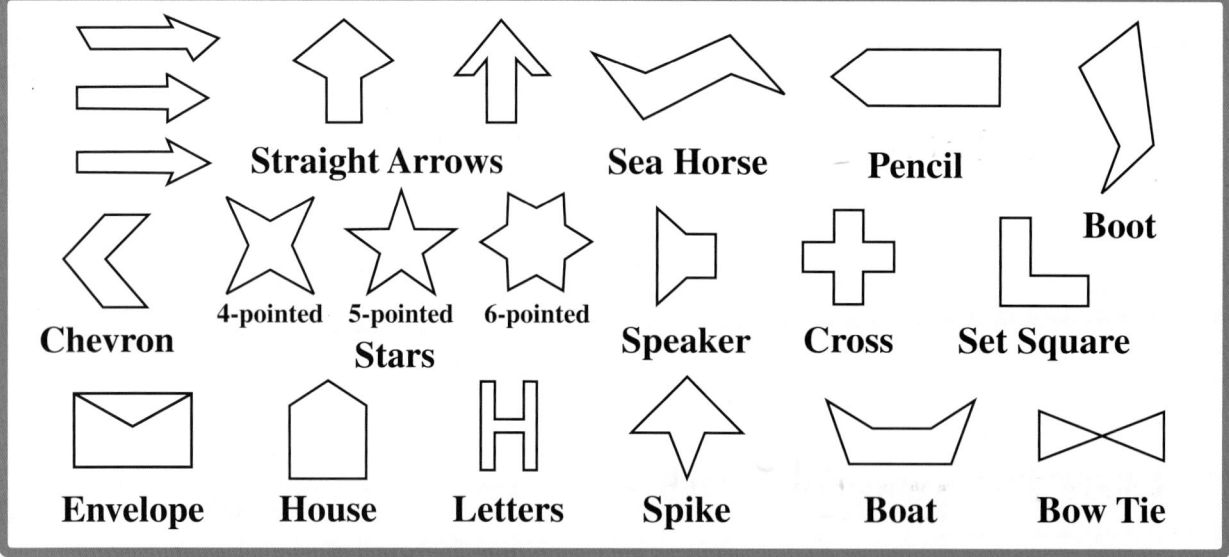

Straight Arrows · Sea Horse · Pencil · Boot

Chevron · 4-pointed 5-pointed 6-pointed Stars · Speaker · Cross · Set Square

Envelope · House · Letters · Spike · Boat · Bow Tie

(ii) Curved Shapes

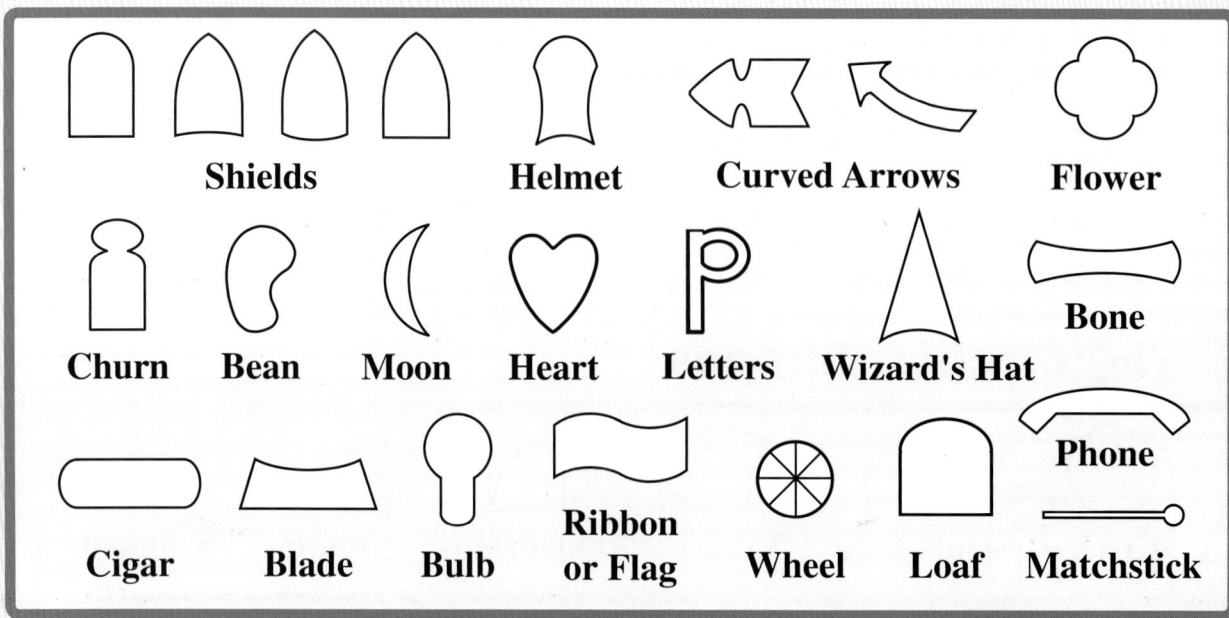

Shields · Helmet · Curved Arrows · Flower

Churn · Bean · Moon · Heart · Letters · Wizard's Hat · Bone

Cigar · Blade · Bulb · Ribbon or Flag · Wheel · Loaf · Phone · Matchstick

c. Naming Shapes

It is important in Non-verbal Reasoning questions to be able to identify and give **Names to Shapes**. It is much easier to describe what is happening to a shape if it is given a name.

(i) Standard Shapes

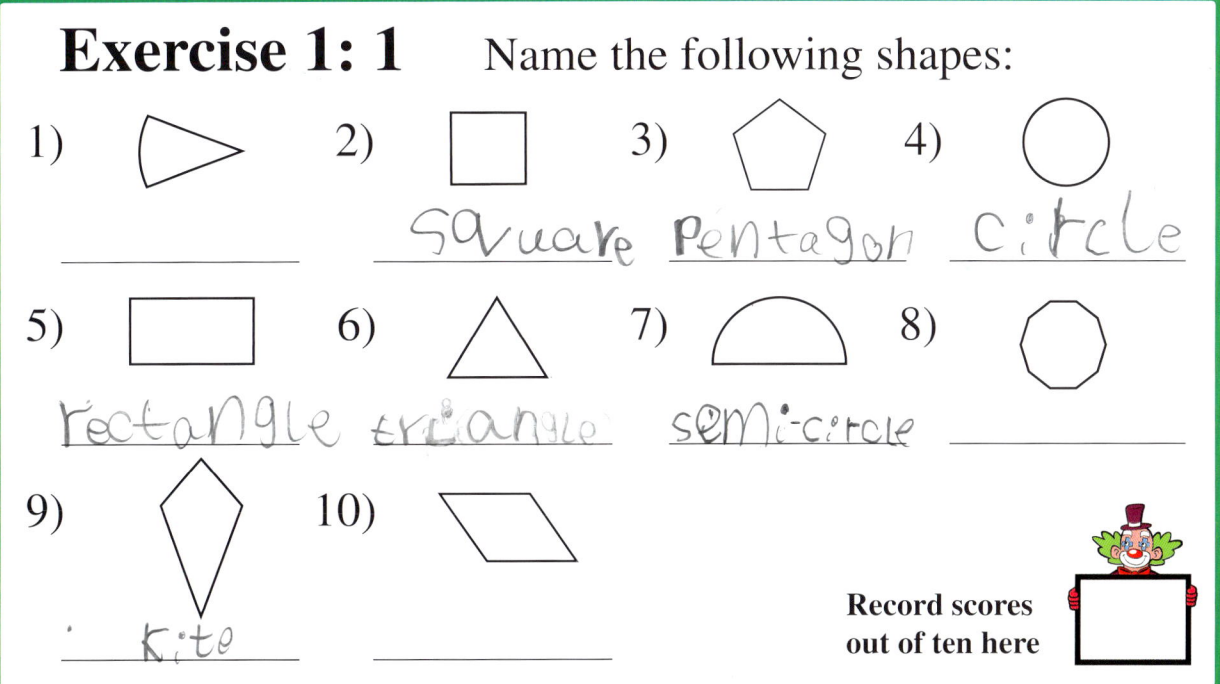

Exercise 1: 1 Name the following shapes:

1) _____ 2) square 3) pentagon 4) circle
5) rectangle 6) triangle 7) semi-circle 8) _____
9) kite 10) _____

Record scores out of ten here

(ii) Specialist Shapes

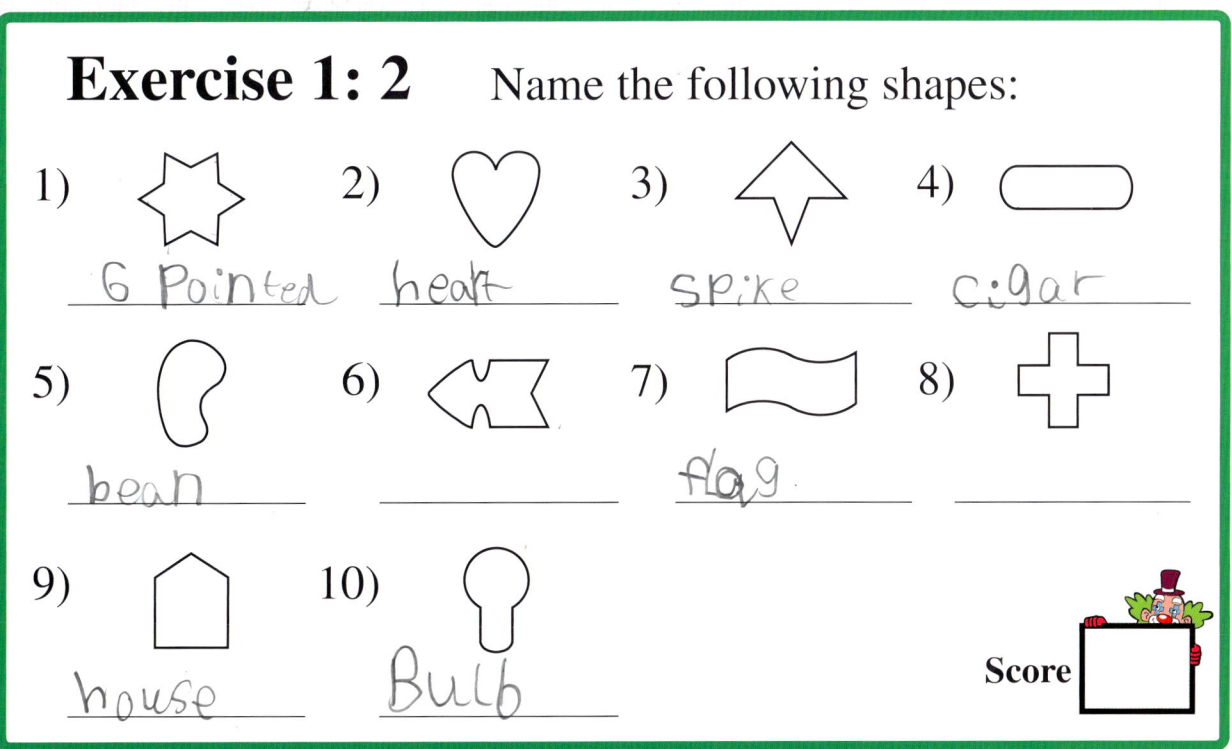

Exercise 1: 2 Name the following shapes:

1) 6 Pointed 2) heart 3) spike 4) cigar
5) bean 6) _____ 7) flag 8) _____
9) house 10) Bulb

Score

d. Shape Questions

Exercise 1: 3   Answer the following:

1) Which is the next shape in the series?

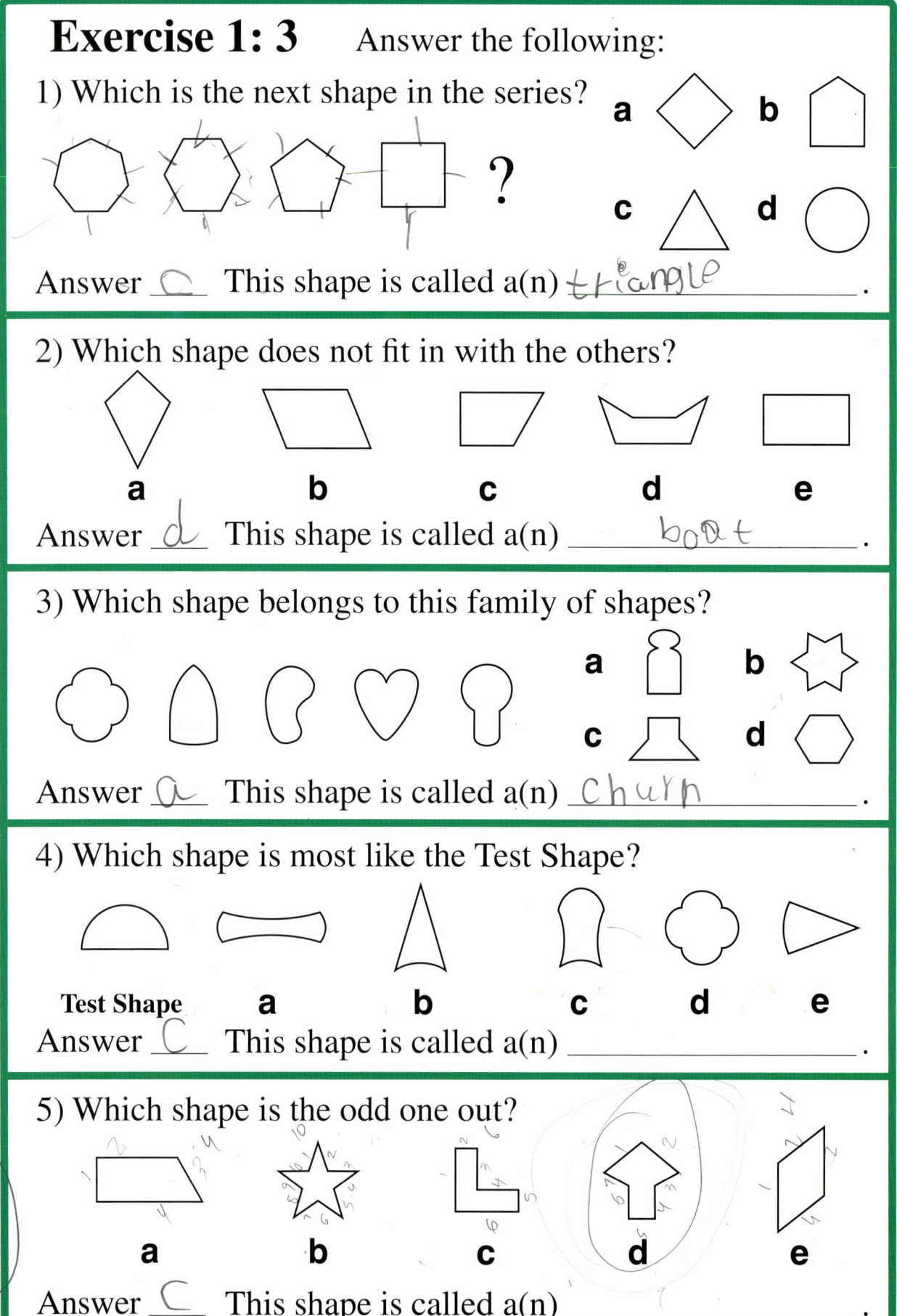

Answer c   This shape is called a(n) triangle.

2) Which shape does not fit in with the others?

Answer d   This shape is called a(n) boat.

3) Which shape belongs to this family of shapes?

Answer a   This shape is called a(n) churn.

4) Which shape is most like the Test Shape?

Answer c   This shape is called a(n) _____.

5) Which shape is the odd one out?

Answer c   This shape is called a(n) _____.

6) Which shape does not fit in with the others?

a   b   c   d   e

Answer __b__ This shape is called a(n) _curved arrow_.

7) Which shape belongs to this family of shapes?

a   b   c   d

Answer __a__ This shape is called a(n) _Shield_.

8) Which shape does not fit in with the others?

a   b   c   d   e

Answer __e__ This shape is called a(n) _hexagon_.

9) Which is the next shape in the series?

a   b   c   d

Answer __b__ This shape is called a(n) _____.

10) Which shape does not fit in with the other shapes?

a   b   c   d   e

Answer __d__ This shape is called a(n) _isosceles_.

Score

Please Complete + Mark

2. Fills
a. Fill Categories

'Closed' shape **Fills** comprise five different categories:
Block • Shaded • Cross-hatched • Liquid • Dotted

b. Fill Palette
(i) Block Fills

| Black  | Grey  | White  |

(ii) Shaded Fills

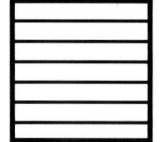 Horizontal Solid Line
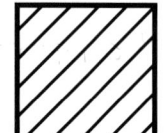 Right Slant Solid Line
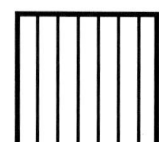 Vertical Solid Line
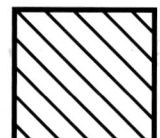 Left Slant Solid Line

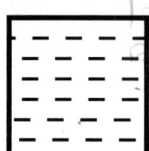 Horizontal Dashed Line
 Right Slant Dashed Line
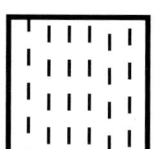 Vertical Dashed Line
 Left Slant Dashed Line

(iii) Cross-hatched Fills

Squares 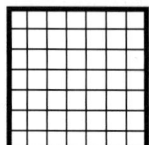   Lattice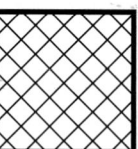

(iv) Liquid Fills

 Speckled   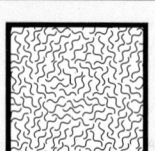 Mottled

(v) Dotted Fills

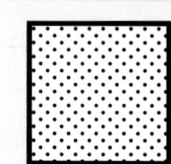 Close   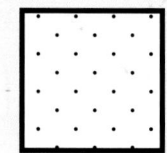 Spaced

c. Naming Fills

> Giving **Names to Fills** also helps when describing shapes.

Exercise 1: 4   Name the following fills:

1) Fill category: __Shaded__
   Fill type: __Right slant solid line__

2) Fill category: __Liquid__
   Fill type: __Mottled__

3) Fill category: __Cross hatched__
   Fill type: __Lattice__

4) Fill category: __Shaded__
   Fill type: __Right slant dashed line__

5) Fill category: __Liquid__
   Fill type: __Speckled__

6) Fill category: __Block__
   Fill type: __Black__

7) Fill category: __Shaded__
   Fill type: __Vertical solid line__

8) Fill category: __Block__
   Fill type: __White__

9) Fill category: __Block__
   Fill type: __Grey__

10) Fill category: __Cross hatched__
    Fill type: __Squared__

Score

d. Fill Questions

Exercise 1: 5   Answer the following:

1) Which shape is next in the series?

Answer __b__
Fill category: __Liquid__   Fill type: __Speckled__

2) Which shape does not fit in with the others?

Answer __c__
Fill category: __cross hatch__   Fill type: __lattice__

3) Which shape is next in the series?

Answer __a__
Fill category: __Shaded__   Fill type: __Left Slant line Solid__

4) Which shape does not fit in with the others?

Answer __b__
Fill category: __Shaded__   Fill type: __Right Slant line Solid__

5) Which shape is next in the series?

Answer __d__
Fill category: __Block__   Fill type: __Black__

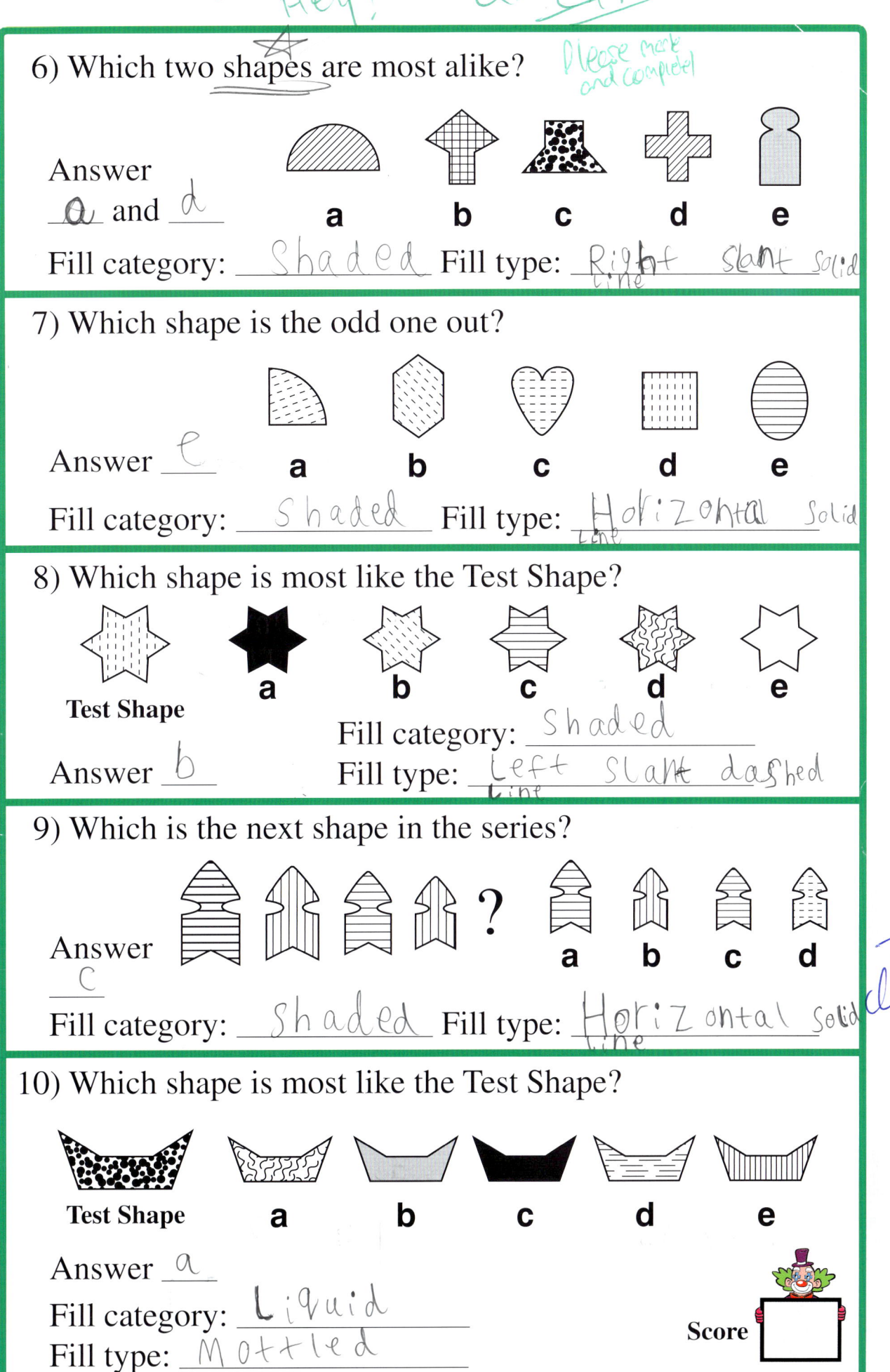

6) Which two shapes are most alike?

Answer a and d

Fill category: Shaded   Fill type: Right slant line solid

7) Which shape is the odd one out?

Answer e

Fill category: Shaded   Fill type: Horizontal line solid

8) Which shape is most like the Test Shape?

Answer b   Fill category: Shaded   Fill type: Left slant line dashed

9) Which is the next shape in the series?

Answer c

Fill category: Shaded   Fill type: Horizontal line solid

10) Which shape is most like the Test Shape?

Answer a
Fill category: Liquid
Fill type: Mottled

3. Lines
a. Lines Palette

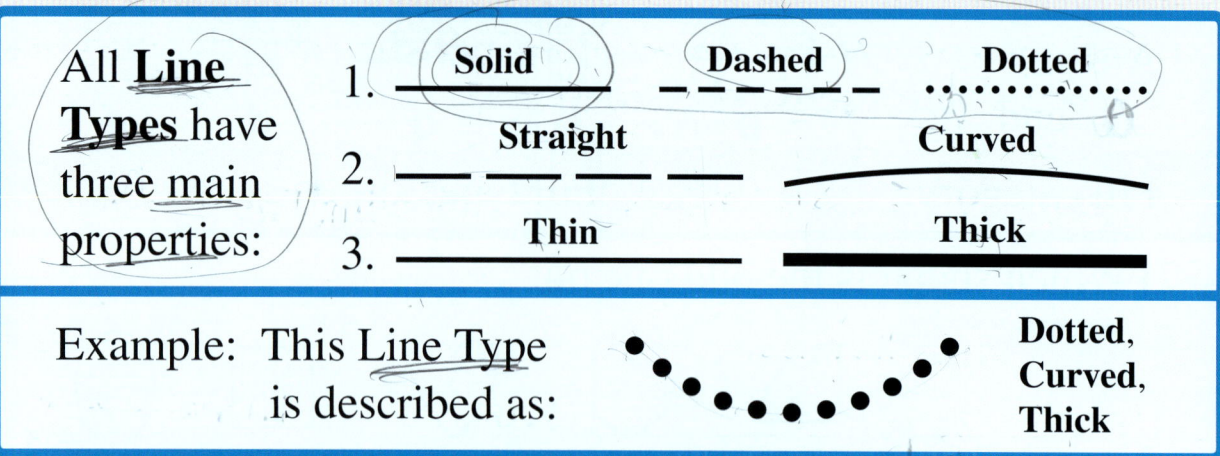

Example: This Line Type is described as: Dotted, Curved, Thick

b. Line Shapes Palette

These comprise everyday recognisable 'open' **Line Shapes**.
Straight-edged Shapes • **Curved Shapes**
This palette is not exhaustive as other shapes do exist.

(i) Straight-edged Shapes

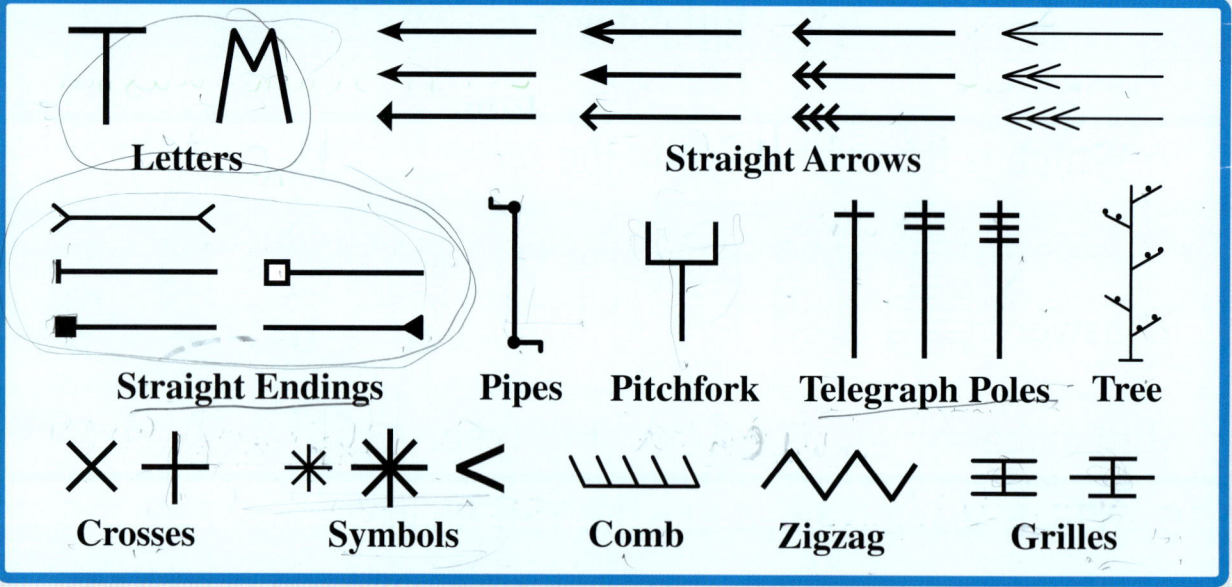

(ii) Curved Shapes

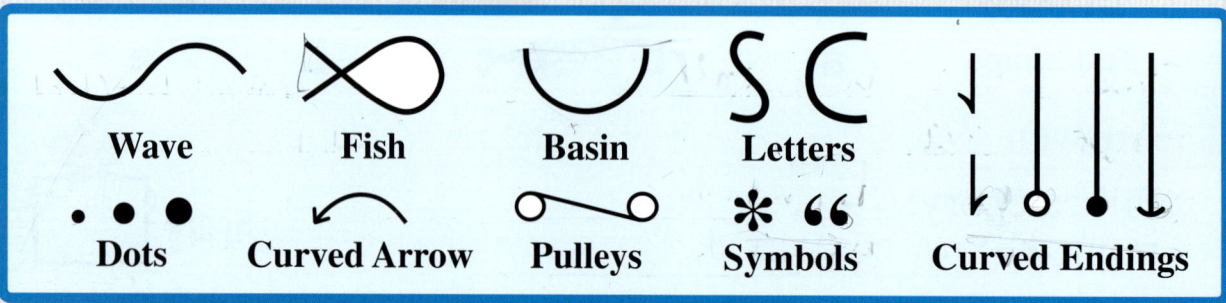

c. Naming Lines

Naming Lines and line shapes helps with identification.

(i) Straight-edged Shapes

Exercise 1: 6a Identify the following line types:

1) Type: Dashed Straight Thin
   Shape: Comb

2) Type: Solid Straight thick
   Shape: Letter

3) Type: Solid Straight thin
   Shape: Straight Arrows

4) Type: dashed Straight thick
   Shape: Zig Zag

5) Type: dotted Straight thin
   Shape: Letter

(ii) Curved Shapes

Exercise 1: 6b Identify the following line types:

6) Type: dotted curved thick
   Shape: Letter

7) Type: dashed curved then
   Shape: Curved Arrow

8) Type: Solid curved thin
   Shape: Wave

9) Type: dash curved thin
   Shape: fish

10) Type: Solid Curved thick
    Shape: Symbols

Score: 9

d. Line Questions

Exercise 1: 7 Answer the following:

1) Which is the next figure in the series?

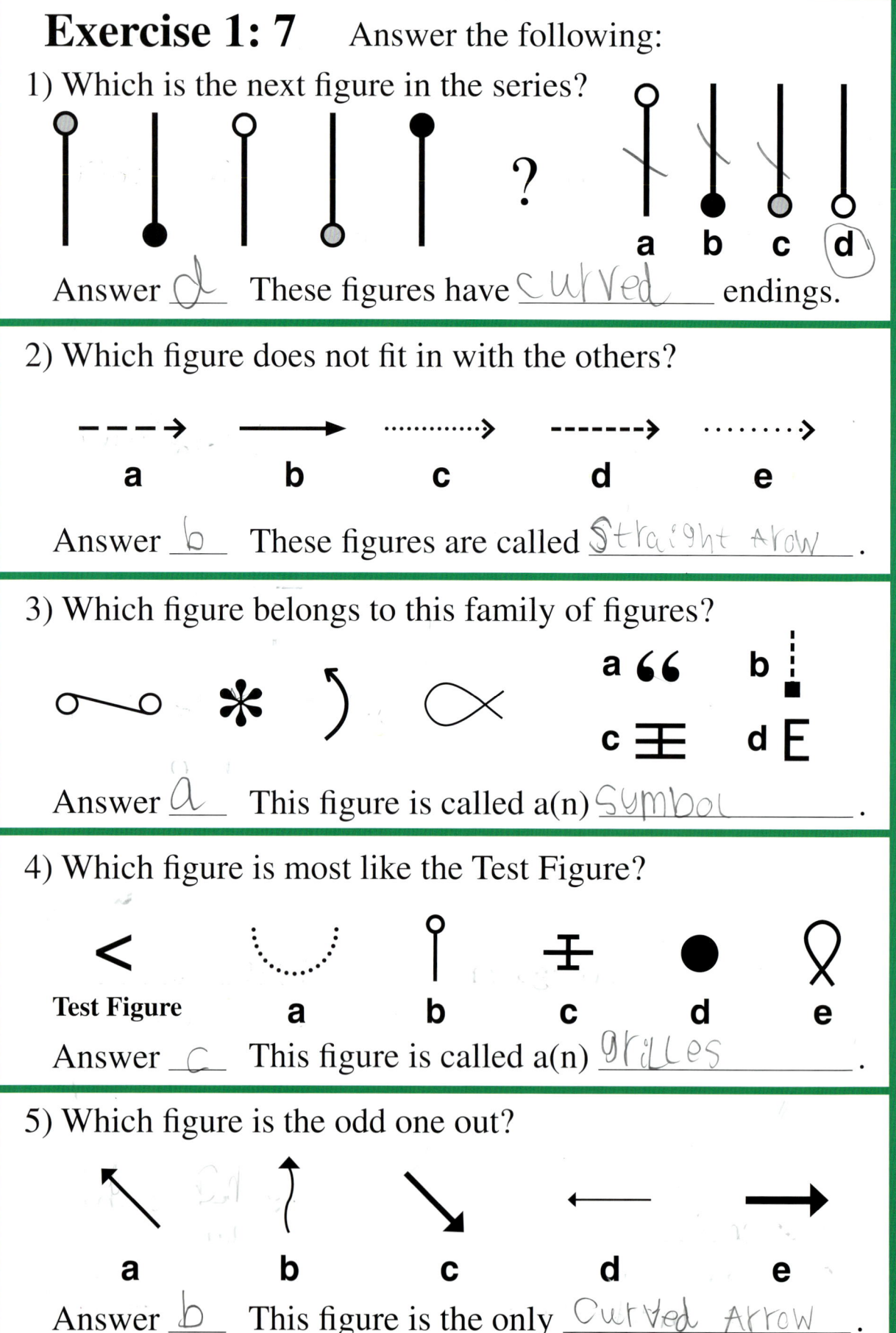

Answer **d** These figures have **curved** endings.

2) Which figure does not fit in with the others?

Answer **b** These figures are called **Straight Arow**.

3) Which figure belongs to this family of figures?

Answer **a** This figure is called a(n) **Symbol**.

4) Which figure is most like the Test Figure?

Answer **c** This figure is called a(n) **grilles**.

5) Which figure is the odd one out?

Answer **b** This figure is the only **Curved Arrow**.

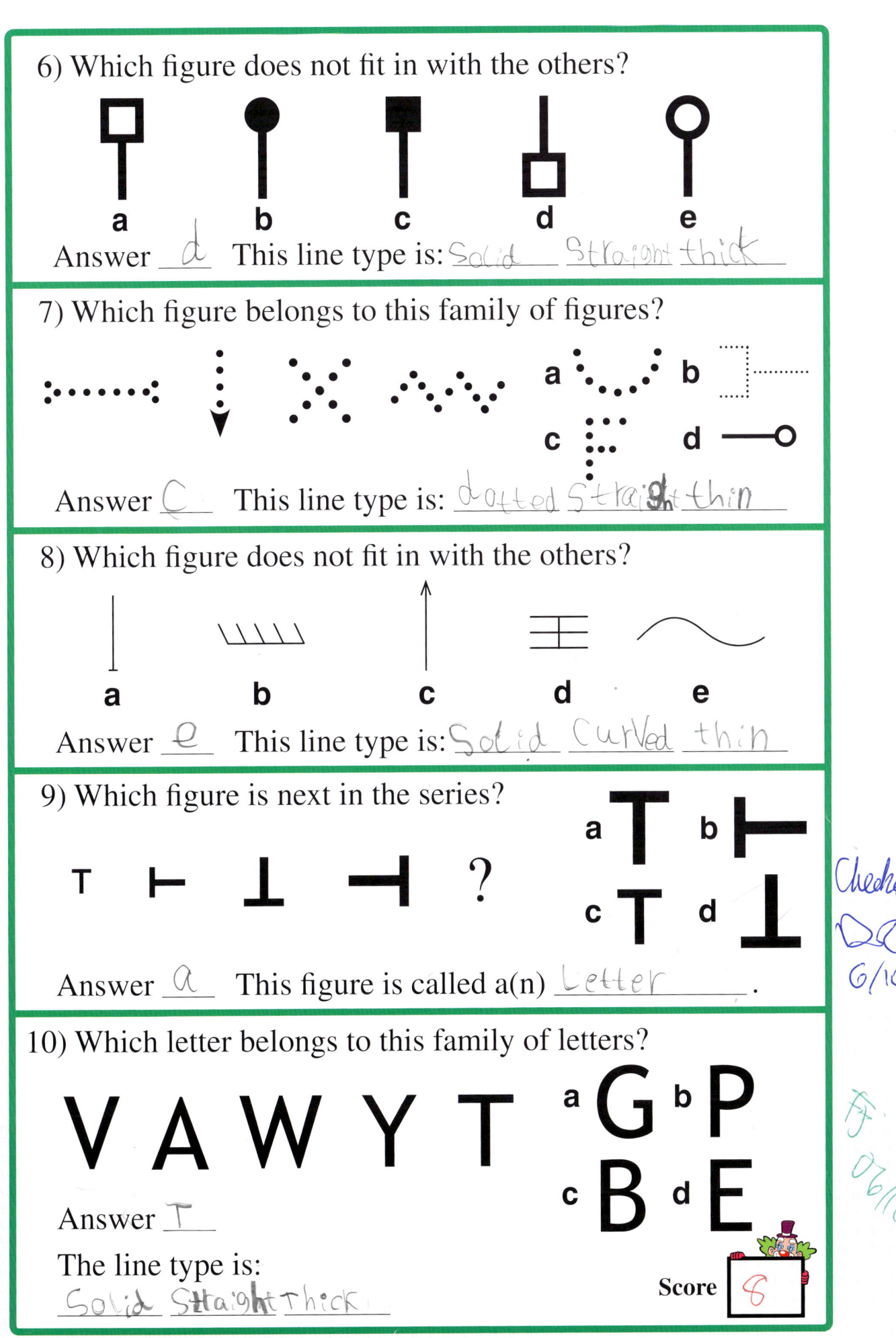

4. Key Questions used in Non-verbal Reasoning

All Non-verbal Reasoning questions are centred around just three key areas. It is important to be able to identify:

Similarity • Difference • Pattern

These questions have already been used in this book:
1) Which shape is most similar to the shape given?
2) Which shape is most different from the shape given?
3) Which shape is the next shape in the series?

a. Similarity

Shapes are **Similar** if they are like each other in some way. This likeness can apply to any aspect of the shape or shapes.

These two shapes are identical, except they are of a different size and fill type. The second shape has also been rotated 45° in a Clockwise direction in relation to the first shape.

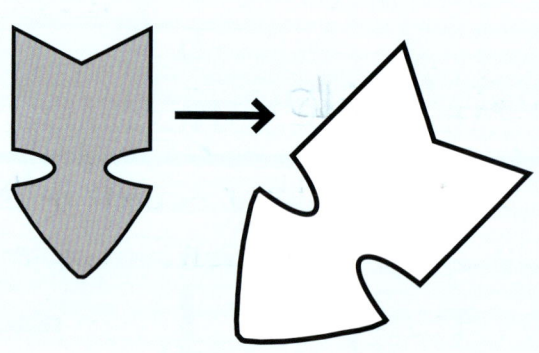

Similarity involves identifying one or more common characteristics between shapes.

Example: Which shape is most similar to the Test Shape?

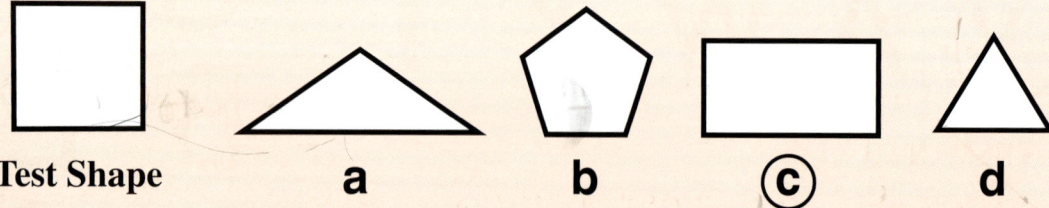

Test Shape   a   b   ⓒ   d

Answer: Shape **c** is most similar as it has four sides.

b. Difference

Shapes are **Different** if they are unlike each other in some way. Difference can mean the shape or shapes have no likeness at all, or there are one or more aspects not alike.

Both these shapes are Stars with the same fill type but they have a different number of sides.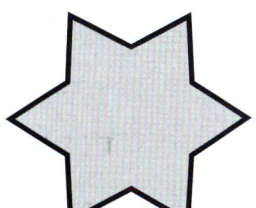

Difference involves spotting the shape most unlike the rest.

Example: Which shape is different from the other shapes?

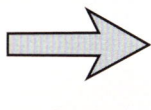 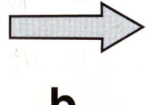 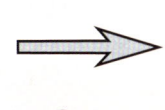  

   a   b   c   ⓓ   e

Answer: Shape **d** is different because it has a Black Fill.

c. Pattern

A **Repetitive** or **Cumulative Pattern** can be established in a series or sequence of shapes or figures (see pages 44-49).

The fill changes from Grey to White to Grey to White repetitively. One more Circle with a Black Fill is added each time **cumulatively**.

   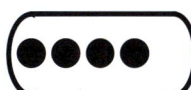 

A pattern is identified by spotting repetition or cumulation.

Example: Which shape is next in the series?

   ?   a   b

Answer: Shape **c** is next because it is bigger and it has a White Fill.   ⓒ    d

Exercise 1: 8   Answer the following:

1) Which is the next shape in the series?

   Answer __C__   Why? _because the order is mottled peckled grey_

2) Which shape does not fit in with the others?

   a   b   c   d   e

   Answer __e__   Why not? _e is diagonel but the nothers are not_

3) Which shape is next in the series?

   Answer __a__   Why? _its black a it has seven sides._

4) Which shape does not fit in with the others?

   a   b   c   d   e

   Answer __b__   Why not? _because it is curved._

5) Which is the next shape in the series?

   a   b   c   d

   Answer ____   Why? ____

B

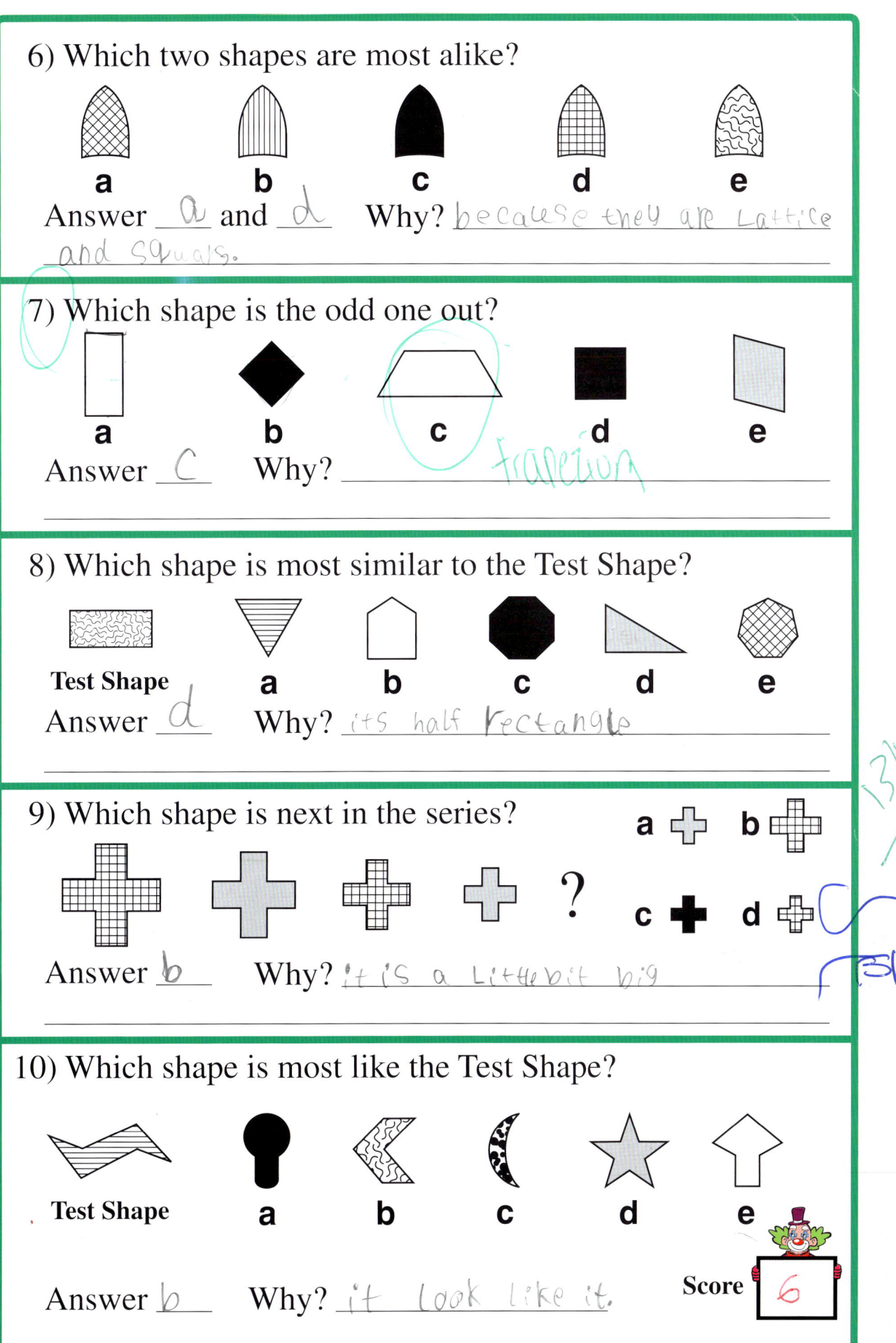

Chapter Two
MOVEMENTS

In Non-verbal Reasoning, shapes can **Move** in four ways:
Reflection • Rotation • Superimposition • Transposition

1. Reflection

A shape can be **Reflected** across an imaginary Mirror Line or Line of Reflection. Shape **A** is reflected the other side of the Mirror Line to form shape **B**.

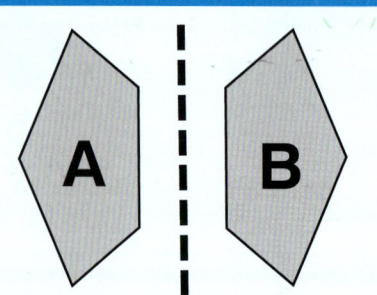

Key Non-verbal Reasoning questions apply to reflections:

Example 1: Which shape is a reflection of the Test Shape?

Test Shape   a   b   ⓒ   d   e

Answer: **c** is a reflection of the Test Shape.

Example 2: Which pair of shapes are not reflections?

a   ⓑ   c   d

Answer: **b** - The Slanted Shaded Fills are not reflections.

Example 3: Which is the next shape in the series?

?   a b ⓒ d

Answer: **c** - The shape reflects correctly and has the correct Liquid Fill type.

© 2011 Stephen Curran

Exercise 2: 1   Answer the following:

1) Which is the next figure in the series?

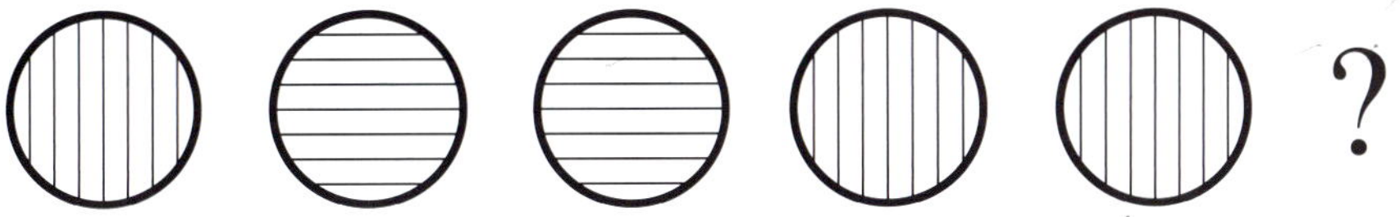

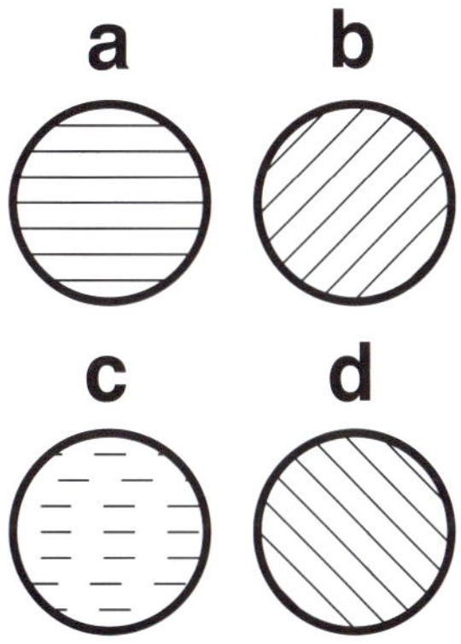

Answer _a_   Fill category: _shaded_
Fill type: _horizantle_
solid line

2) Which pair of shapes does not fit in with the others?

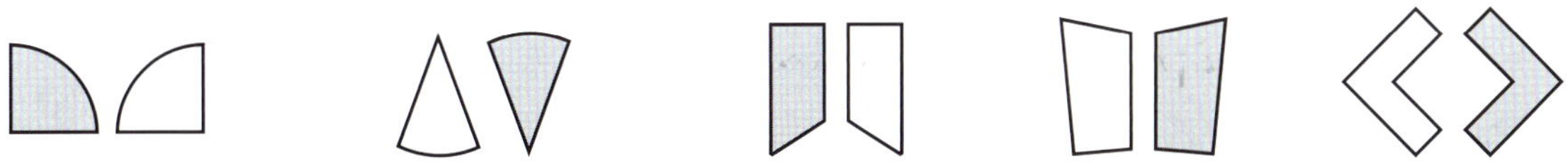

Answer _b_   These shapes are called _Sector_.

3) Which is the next figure in the series?

Answer _a_   Fill categories: _block_ _Shade_
Fill types: _black_ _vertical_
solid line

4) Which figure does not fit in with the others?

Answer _b_   Why not? _they are not reflect_

5) Which letter is next in the series?

D E H I M O T ?

Answer _a_   Why? _____

6) Which two pairs of shapes are most alike?

a   b   c   d   e

Answer __a__ and __e__   Why? they are same and looking at each other

7) Which pair of shapes is the odd one out?

a   b   c   d   e

Annotations: different hills; same; hills same; rotate 180; changed reflection; hills change

Answer __c__   i) Why? only reflection where hills stay same

ii) These shapes are called _____.

8) Which figure is a reflection of the Test Figure?

Test Figure   a   b   c   d   e

Annotations: wrong hill; should be black; wrong way; wrong way; slanted; 2 sides equal other 2 sides equal

Answer __d__   The inner shape is called a(n) __parallelogram__.

9) Which is the next shape in the series?

Annotations: same shape; rotate 180; same hill; same shape rotate 180; position down; black & reversed; hang up

a   b   c   d

Answer __c__   What is this shape called? _____

10) Which figure is a reflection of the Test Figure?

Test Figure   a   b   c   d   e

Annotations: wrong way; wrong way; wrong way

Answer __e__   The outer shape is called a(n) _____.

Score: 20/10
STOP   A-9 20/10

2. Rotations

In Non-verbal Reasoning, shapes can **Rotate** in a Clockwise or Anticlockwise direction.

To avoid confusion it is best to measure the rotation by the shortest route. This will be in either a **Clockwise** or an **Anticlockwise** direction around the **360°** turn. There are three main rotations:

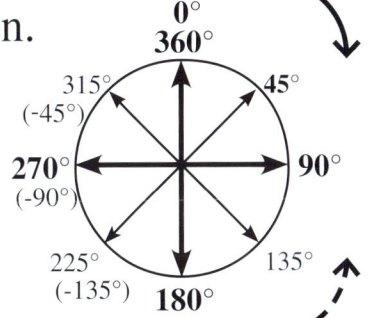

45° ($\frac{1}{8}$) turn   90° ($\frac{1}{4}$) turn   180° ($\frac{1}{2}$) turn

Smaller shapes can rotate around the outside of larger shapes or on the inside of larger shapes.

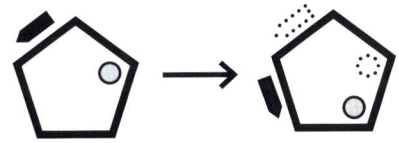

The Pencil Shape has moved Anticlockwise around the Pentagon and the Circle has moved Clockwise within the Pentagon.

Key Non-verbal Reasoning questions apply to rotations:

Example 1: Which shape completes the second pair of shapes?

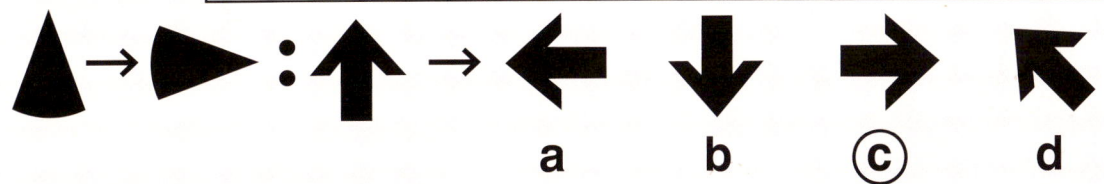

Answer: **c** - It has rotated 90° Clockwise (in the same way as the first pair).

Example 2: Which rotation is the odd one out?

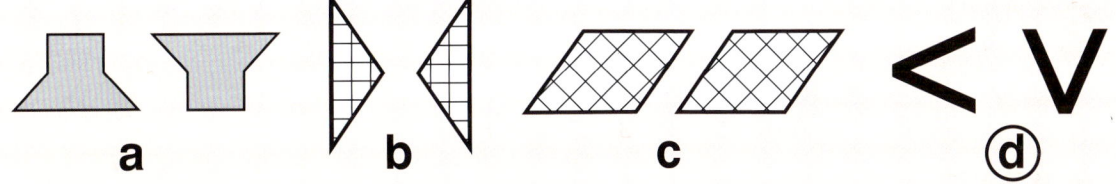

Answer: **d** - It has rotated 90° Anticlockwise but should rotate 180°.

Example 3: Which figure is next in the series?

Answer: **d** - The Arrow rotates 45° Anticlockwise; the next Arrow must have a Black Fill; the Circle rotates 45° Clockwise around the centre (or 90° Clockwise around the Arrow).

Exercise 2: 2   Answer the following:

1) Which is the next figure in the series?

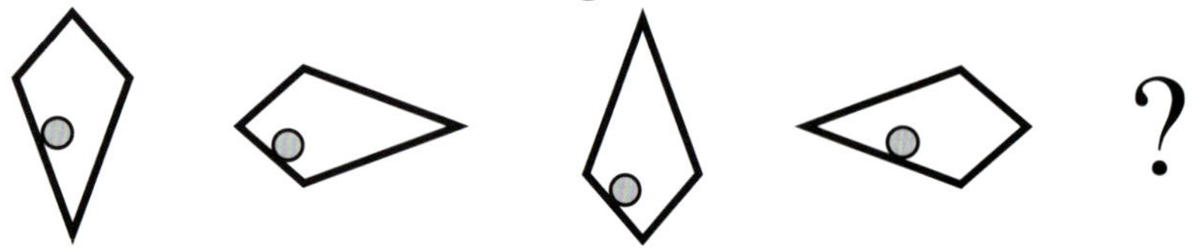

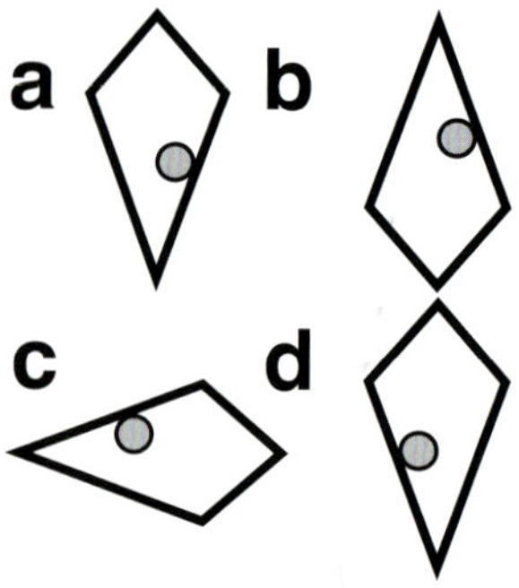

Answer ____   The Kite has been rotated Anticlockwise ____°.

The Circle rotates around the Kite in a(n) _____ direction.

2) Which pair of shapes does not rotate like the Test Shapes?

Test Shapes   a   b   c

Answer _a_   The shape has been rotated _90_° _a(c ow_ .

3) Which shape rotates in the same way as the Test Shapes?

Test Shapes   a   b   c

Answer _a_   The shape has been rotated ____°.

4) Which figure is most like the Test Figure?

Test Figure   a   b   c   d

Answer ____   In comparison with the outer shape the inner shapes have rotated ____° and ____°.

5) Which figure is the odd one out?

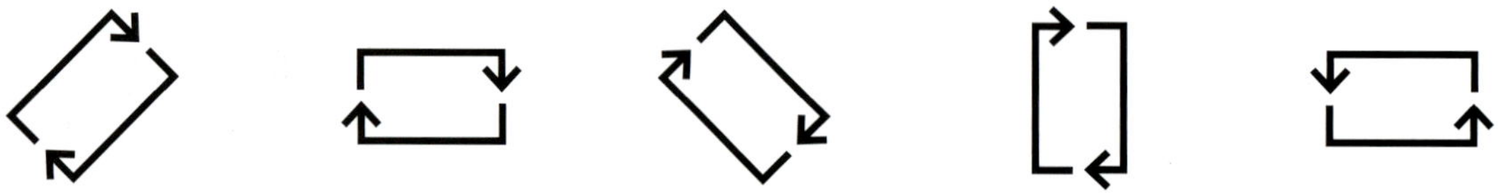

a   b   c   d   e

Answer ____   It rotates in a(n) _____ direction.

6) Which figure does not fit in with the other figures?

   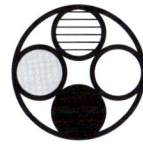 
    a   b   c   d   e

Answer _____ Why not? _____

7) Which shape belongs to this family of shapes?

   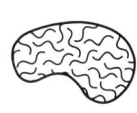   
                                                      a   b

                        Why? _____   c   d

Answer _____ _____

8) Which pair of shapes does not rotate like the Test Shapes?

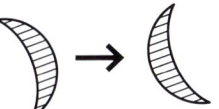   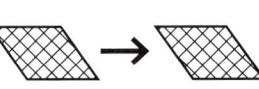   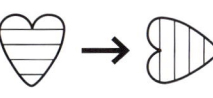   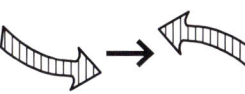

Test Shapes   a   b   c

Answer _____ This shape has been rotated _____°.

9) Which figure is next in the series?

       a    b

                                                                        c    d

Answer _____ The Star rotates _____°.

The shading rotates _____° in a(n) _____ direction.

10) Which letter is missing from this family of letters?

H I O S X   a P   b Y

                                                              c G   d N

Answer _____ Why? _____

_____   **Score**

© 2011 Stephen Curran

3. Superimposition

In Non-verbal Reasoning, shapes can be **Superimposed** onto other shapes. These superimpositions can include a **Merger**, an **Overlay**, a **Linkage** or an **Enclosure**.

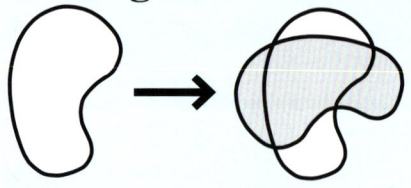 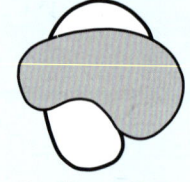 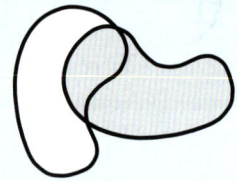 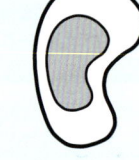

1. Merger   **2. Overlay**   **3. Linkage**   **4. Enclosure**

Superimpositions have been indicated with a Grey Fill to help with visual clarity and ease of understanding.	The second shape Merges (crosses over) the first shape. The integrity (lines) of both shapes is retained. In this case it is a 90° rotation and inversion of the original shape.	The second shape Overlays (is on top of) the first shape. The original shape can be fully or partially covered. In this case it is a 90° rotation of the original shape.	The second shape is Linked to (does not cross over) the first shape. The integrity (lines) of both shapes is kept. Several shapes can be linked together.	The second shape is Enclosed within the first shape. In this case a copy of the first shape is reduced in size and enclosed within the original shape.

Key Non-verbal Reasoning questions use superimpositions:

Example 1: Which figure is most similar to the Test Figure?

Test Figure   **a**   **b**   **c**   **ⓓ**

Answer: **d** - This is a rotated superimposed merger of 90°.

Example 2: Which superimposition is the odd one out?

a   **b**   **ⓒ**   **d**   **e**

Answer: **c** - The enclosed shape has not been rotated 180°.

Example 3: Which superimposition is next in the series?

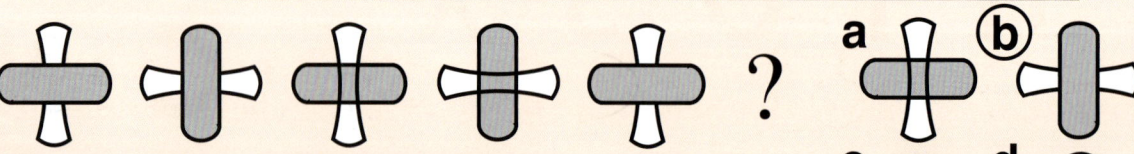

Answer: **b** - The previous figure has been rotated 90°. The Cigar Shape with a Grey Fill overlays the Bone Shape.

Exercise 2: 3   Answer the following:

1) Which is the next figure in the series?

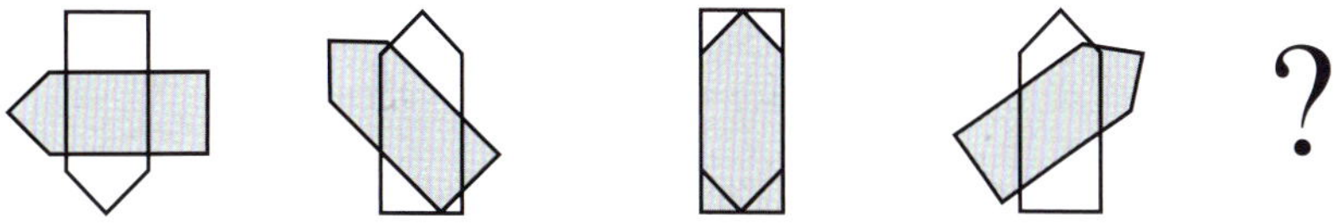

Answer ____   Superimposition type: _____

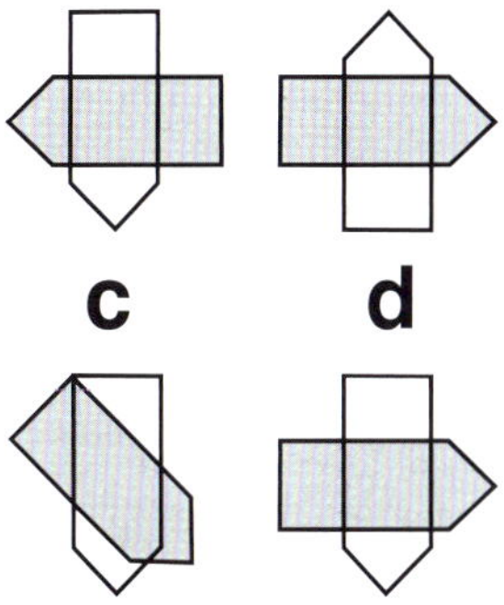

2) Which figure does not fit in with the others?

a   b   c   d   e

Answer ____   Superimposition type: _____

3) Which figure belongs to this family of figures?

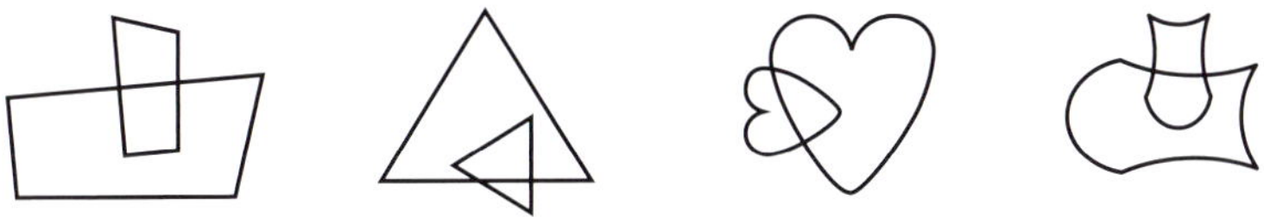

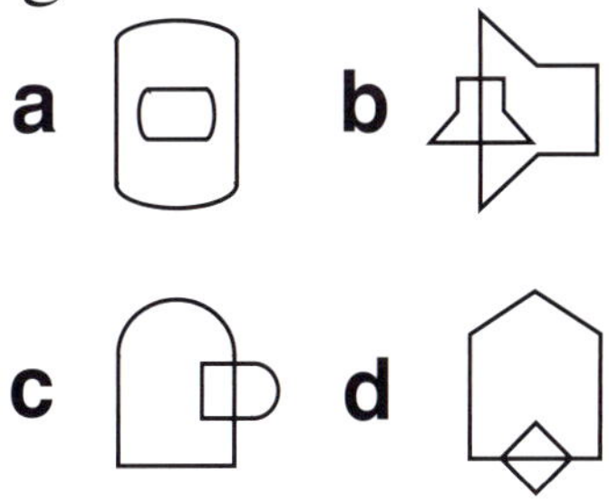

Answer ____   Superimposition type: _____

4) Which figure is most like the Test Figure?

Test Figure   a   b   c   d

Answer ____   Superimposition type: _____

5) Which figure is the odd one out?

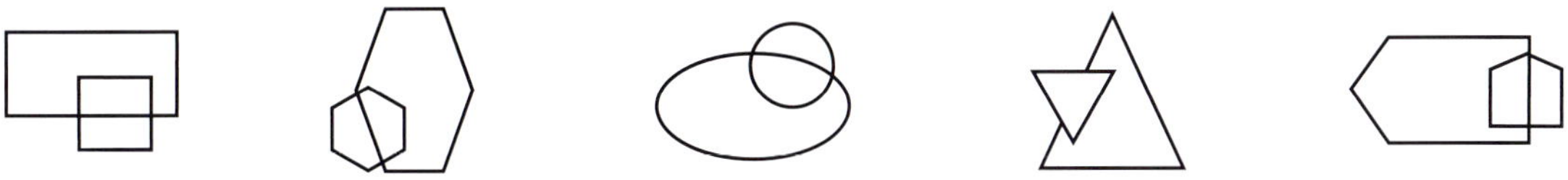

a   b   c   d   e

Answer ____   Superimposition type: _____

© 2011 Stephen Curran

6) Which figure does not fit in with the others?

a    b   c   d

Answer ____

Superimposition types: _____ and _____

7) Which figure belongs to this family of figures?

a   b   c   d

Answer ____   Superimposition type: _____

8) Which figure does not fit in with the other figures?

a   b   c   d   e

Answer ____   Superimposition type: _____

9) Which figure is next in the series?

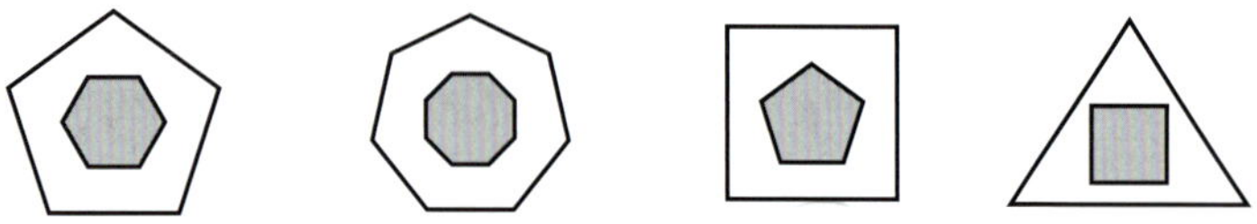

a   b   c   d

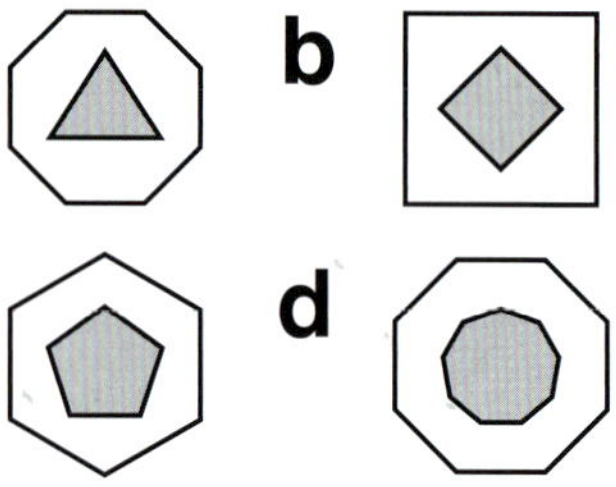

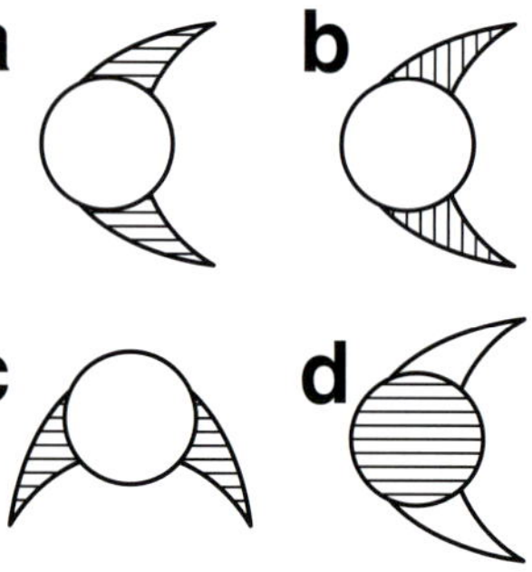

Superimposition type: _____

Answer ____

10) Which figure belongs to this family of figures?

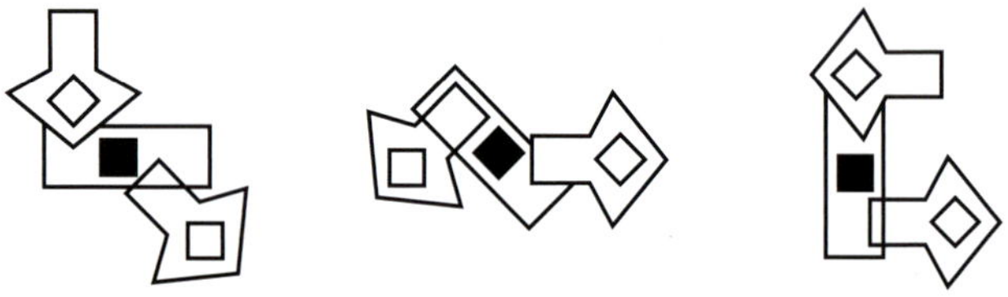

a   b   c   d

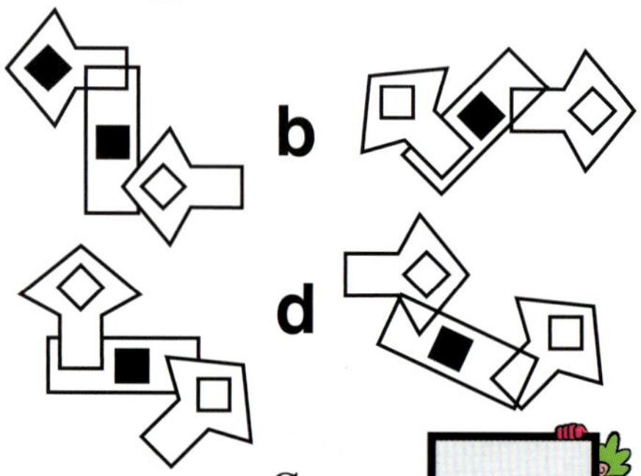

Answer ____

Superimposition types: _____ / _____ / _____

Score ____

4. Transposition

In Non-verbal Reasoning, shapes can be **Transposed** or **Moved** from one position to another, either Horizontally or Vertically. Movements to the right or to the left are Horizontal and movements up or down are Vertical. Some transpositions involve both Vertical and Horizontal movements, i.e. a shape could move up and to the right.

Transpositions are enclosed to show movement.

1. Horizontal Transposition

2. Vertical Transposition

3. Horizontal and Vertical Transposition

Key Non-verbal Reasoning questions use transpositions:

Example 1: Which figure is most similar to the Test Figure?

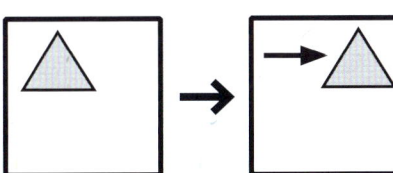  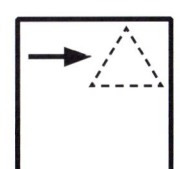 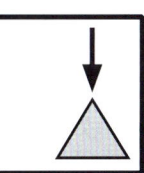

Test Figure   a   b   c

Answer: **b** - It is a vertical and horizontal transposition.

Example 2: Which transposition is the odd one out?

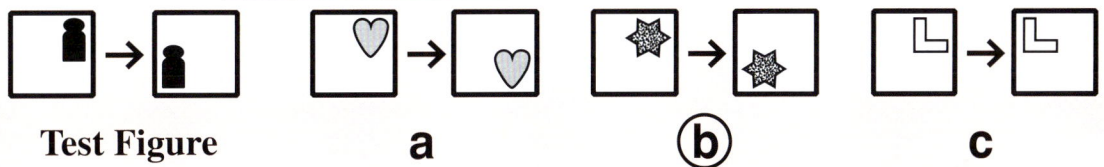

a   b   c   d

Answer: **a** - It is a horizontal transposition.

Example 3: Which transposition is next in the series?

Answer: **c** - The Hexagon changes to a Grey Fill and transposes vertically.

Exercise 2: 4   Answer the following:

1) Which figure is next in the series?

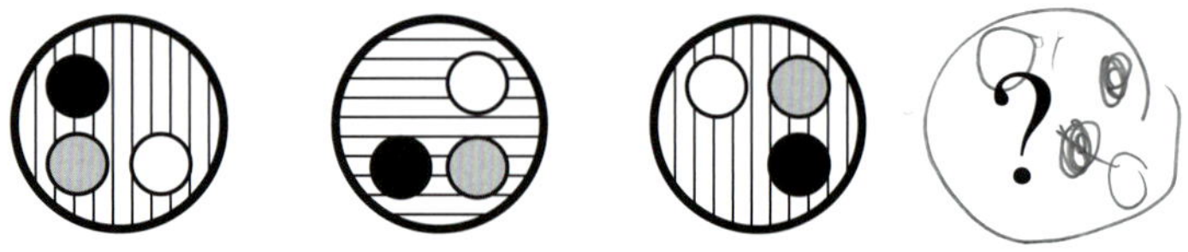

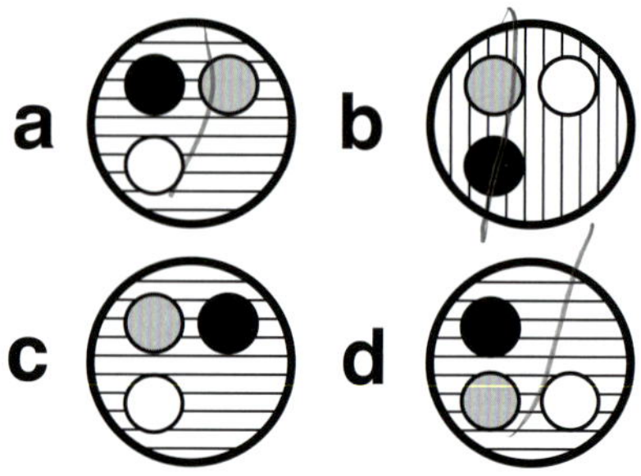

Answer ____   Transposition types:

Black Fill: _Vertical_   White: _____   Grey: _____

2) Which figure completes the second pair of figures?

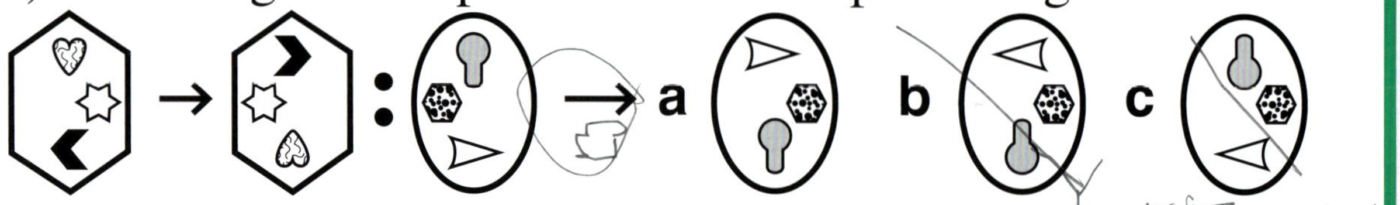

Answer _b_   Transposition types: Hexagon: _horizontil_
Wizard's Hat: _verthicl_   Bulb: _____

3) Which is the next figure in the series?

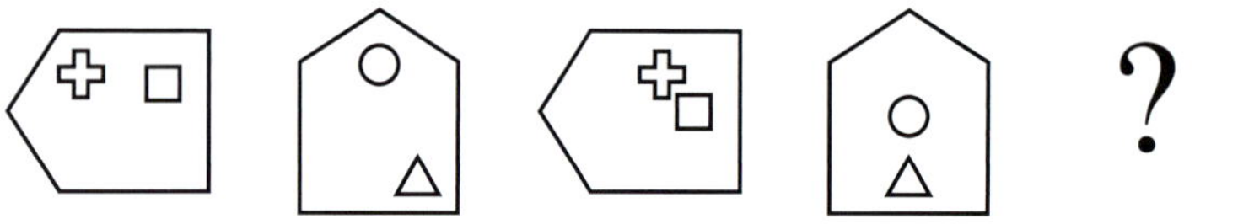

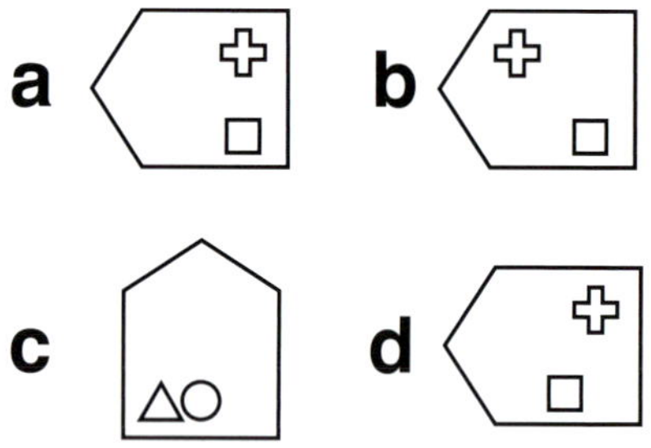

Answer ____   Transposition types:
Cross: _____   Square: _____

4) Which pair of figures does not fit in with the others?

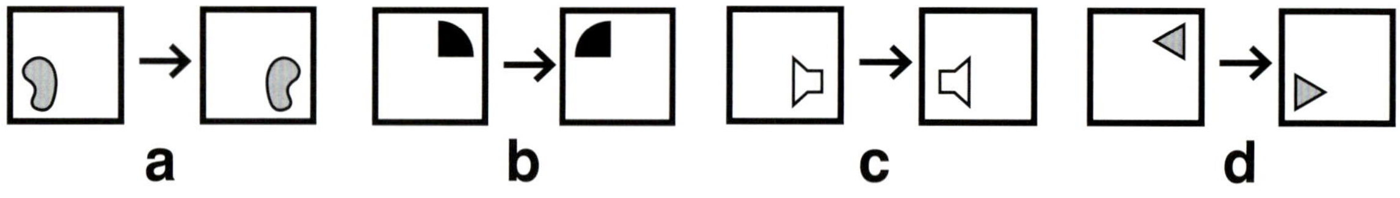

Transposition type:
Answer ____   _____ and _____

5) Which is the next figure in the series?

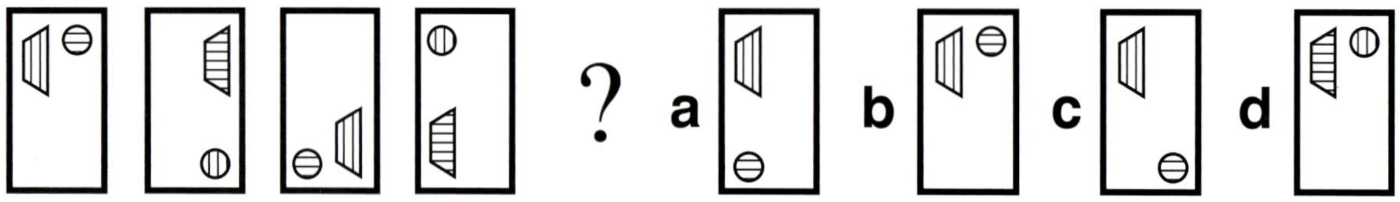

Answer ____   Transposition types: Circle: _____
Isosceles Trapezium: _____

30   © 2011 Stephen Curran

6) Which figure completes the second pair of figures?

Answer ____ Transposition types: Pulley: _____
T Shape: _____ and _____

7) Which pair of figures is the odd one out?

Answer ____ Transposition type: _____

8) Which pair of figures is most like the Test Figures?

Answer ____ Transposition types:
Square: _____ Star: _____

9) Which figure is next in the series?

Answer ____
Transposition type: _____

10) Which pair of figures is most like the Test Figures?

Answer ____
Transposition types:
_____ and _____

Score

Chapter Three
MANIPULATIONS

In Non-verbal Reasoning, shapes can be **Manipulated** by:
Size • **Addition** • **Subtraction** • **Frequency**

1. Size

Shapes can **Increase** in size or **Decrease** in size:

1. Enlargement    2. Reduction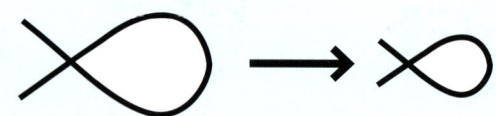

Key Non-verbal Reasoning questions apply to size change:

Example 1: Which shape completes the second pair of shapes?

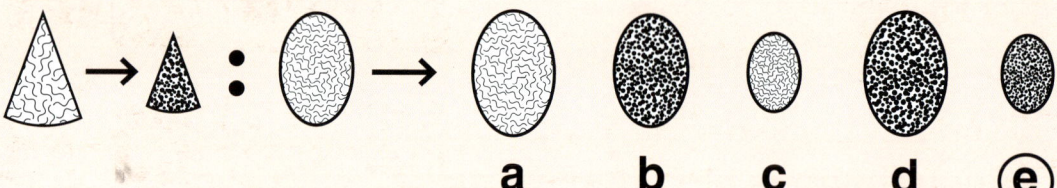

Answer: Shape **e** is a reduction and has a Speckled Fill.

Example 2: Which shape is different from the others?

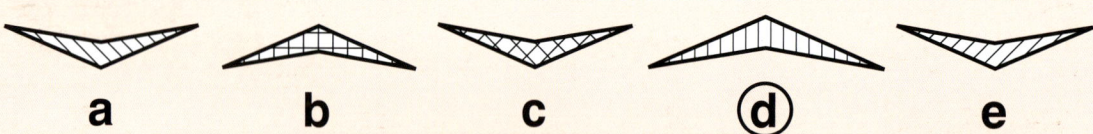

Answer: Shape **d** is an enlargement of the other shapes.

Example 3: Which shape is next in the series?

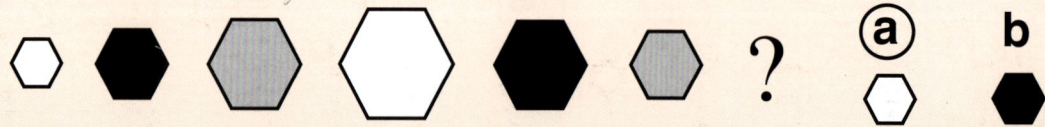 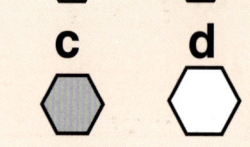

Answer: Shape **a** is a reduction (the next smallest) and has the correct fill.

Exercise 3: 1   Answer the following:

1) Which is the next shape in the series?

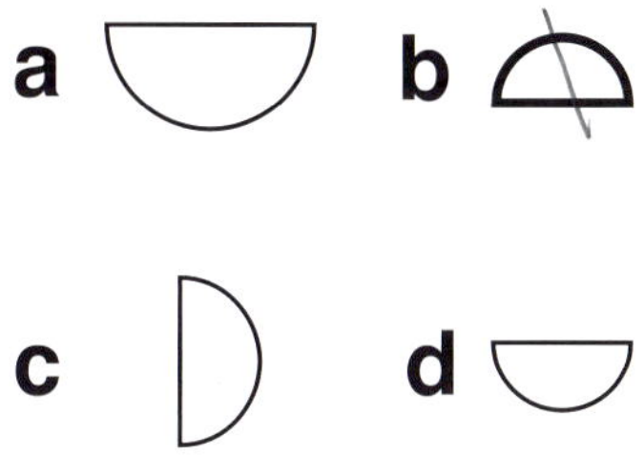

Answer __d__

The change of size is a(n) __Reduction__.

2) Which shape does not fit in with the others?

Answer __e__   The change of size is a(n) __Redution__.

3) Which pair of figures is most similar to the Test Figures?

Test Figures

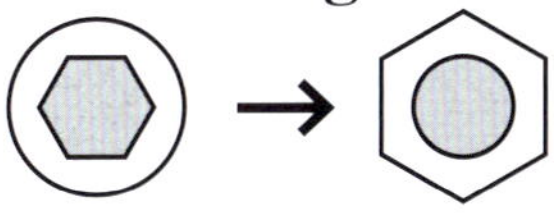

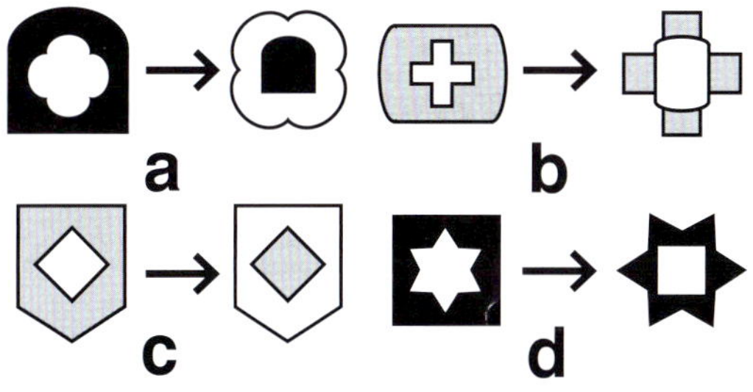

Answer ____   Name the shapes:
The _____ shape reduces.
The _____ shape enlarges.

4) Which pair of figures is most like the Test Figures?

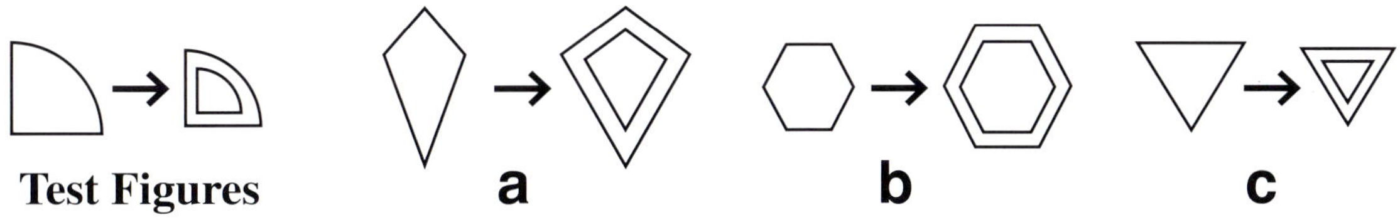

Test Figures

Answer ____   The change of size is a(n) _____.

5) Which is the next figure in the series?

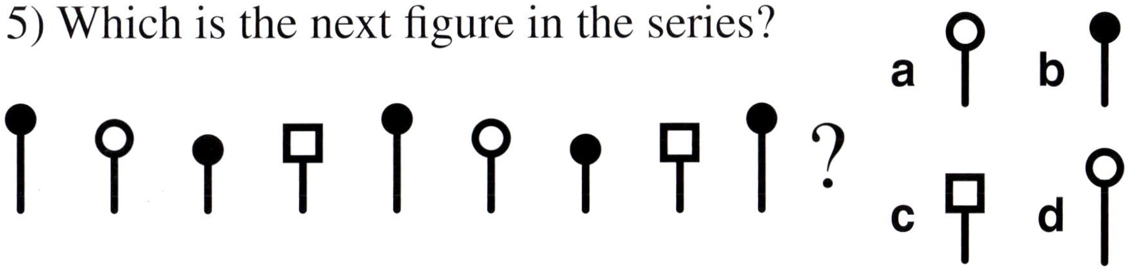

Answer ____   The change of size is a(n) _____.

6) Which pair of figures does not fit in with the other figures?

a   b   c   d

Answer ____   The change of size is a(n) _____.

7) Which figure belongs to this family of figures?

a   b   c   d

Answer ____

The outer shape is a(n) _____ of the enclosed shape.

8) Which figure does not fit in with the others?

a   b   c   d   e

Answer ____   The change of size is a(n) _____.

9) Which figure is the odd one out?

a   b   c

Answer ____   The change of size is a(n) _____.

10) Which figure belongs to this family of figures?

a   b   c   d

Answer ____

If the enclosed Squares are placed in size order, largest to smallest, each one would be a(n) _____ of the previous Square.

Score

2. Addition

In Non-verbal Reasoning, one or more shapes can be **Added** to the original shape or separate additional shapes can be added.

1. Additions to shapes

The original shape has been copied, rotated 90° and superimposed onto the original shape. Additions are often combined with rotations, reflections, superimpositions and inversions.

2. Additional shapes

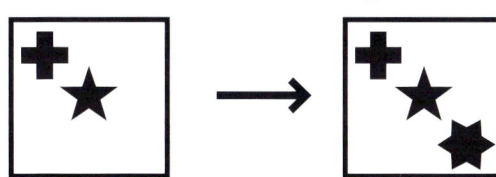

A third shape has been added to the two original shapes. This can also be understood as a change in Frequency (see pages 41-43).

Key Non-verbal Reasoning questions apply to additions:

Example 1: Which shape has an addition to the Test Shape?

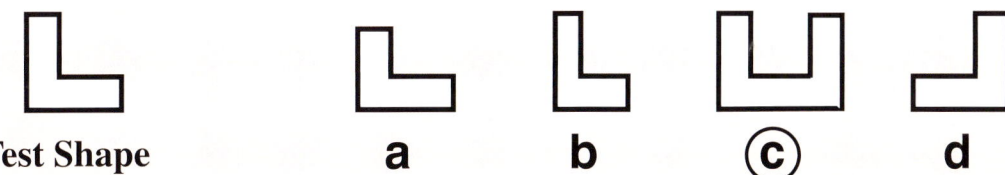

Answer: **c** - The original shape has received an addition.

Example 2: Which shape has no additions to the Test Shape?

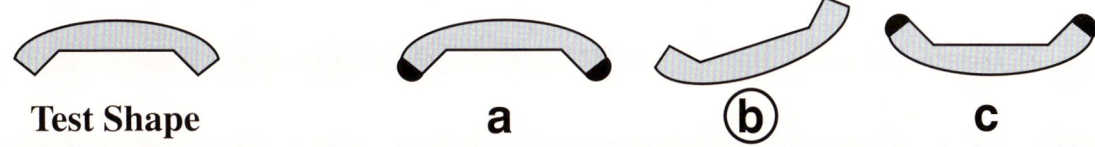

Answer: **b** - The shape has been rotated but has no additions.

Example 3: Which figure is next in the series?

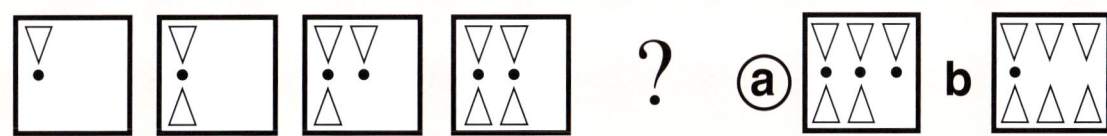

Answer: **a**

This has an addition of one Triangle with a White Fill at the top of the square and one more Circle with a Black Fill in the middle.

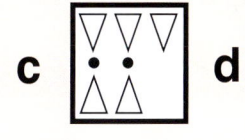

© 2011 Stephen Curran

Exercise 3: 2   Answer the following:

1) Which is the next figure in the series?

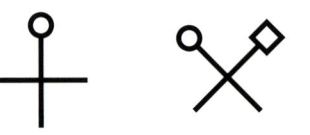 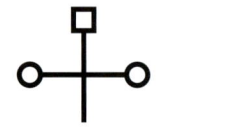 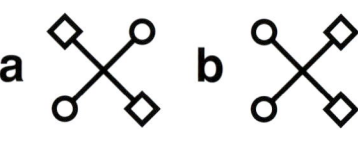
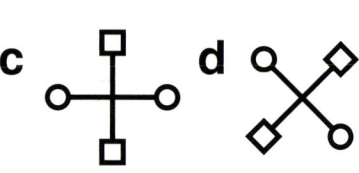

Answer ____
Name the shape that should be added. _____

2) Which pair of figures does not fit in with the others?

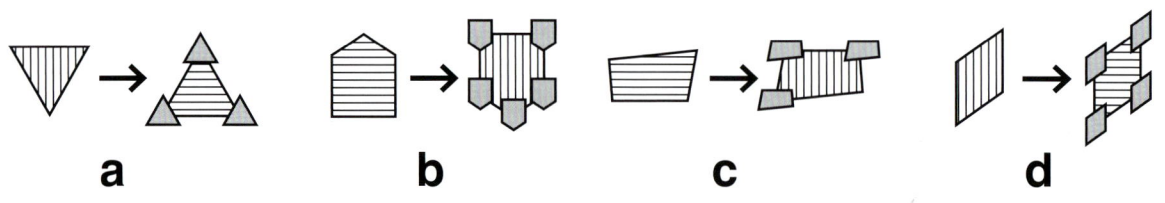

Answer ____   The missing overlay shape is a(n) _____.

3) Which pair of figures belongs to this family of figures?

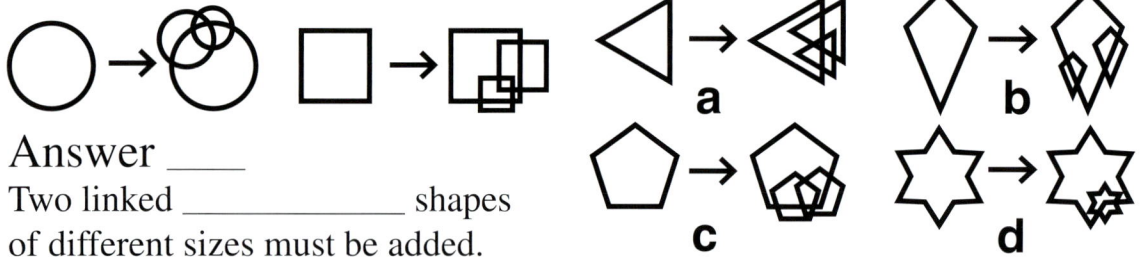

Answer ____
Two linked _____ shapes of different sizes must be added.

4) Which pair of figures is most like the Test Figures?

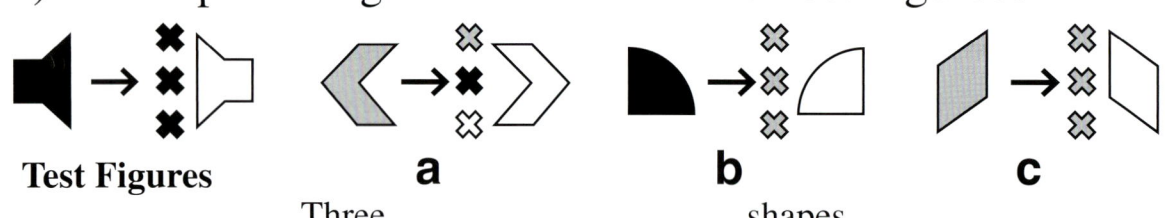

Test Figures

Answer ____   Three _____ shapes with _____ fills must be added.

5) Which pair of figures is the odd one out?

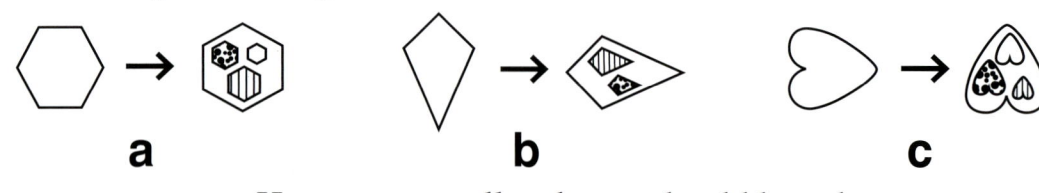

Answer ____   How many smaller shapes should have been added? _____ shape(s)

6) Which pair of figures does not fit in with the other figures?

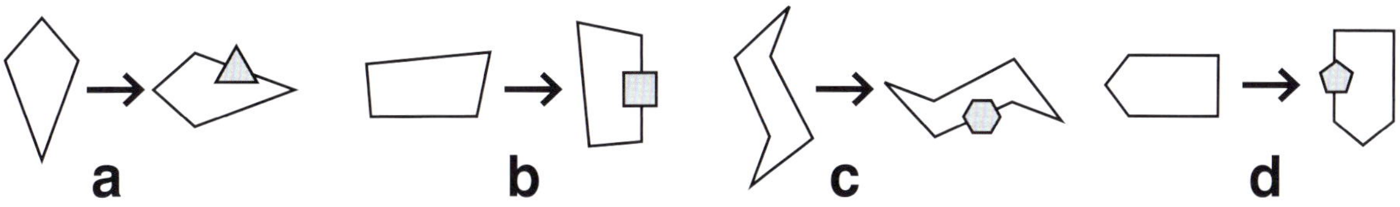

a   b   c   d

Answer _____ The added shape should have _____ sides.

7) Which pair of figures is most like the Test Figures?

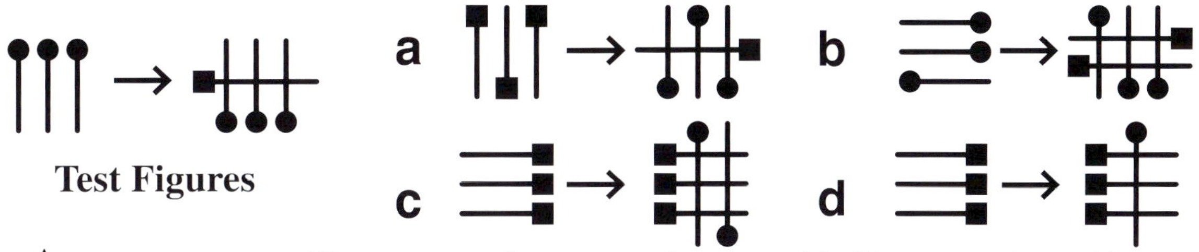

Test Figures

a   b   c   d

Answer _____ How many shapes need to be added? _____ shape(s)

8) Which pair of figures does not fit in with the others?

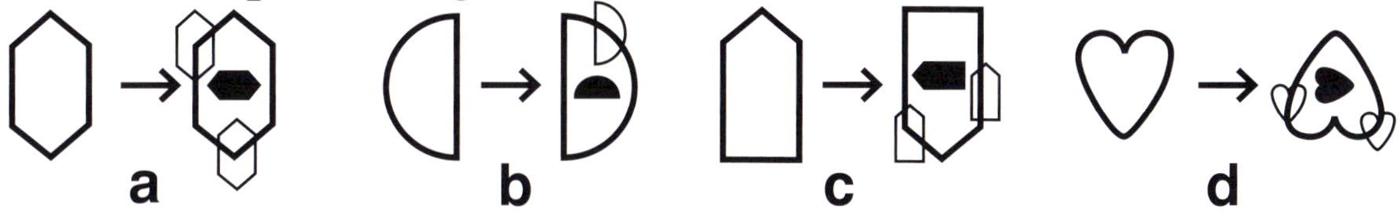

a   b   c   d

Answer _____
Why not? _____

9) Which is the next figure in the series?

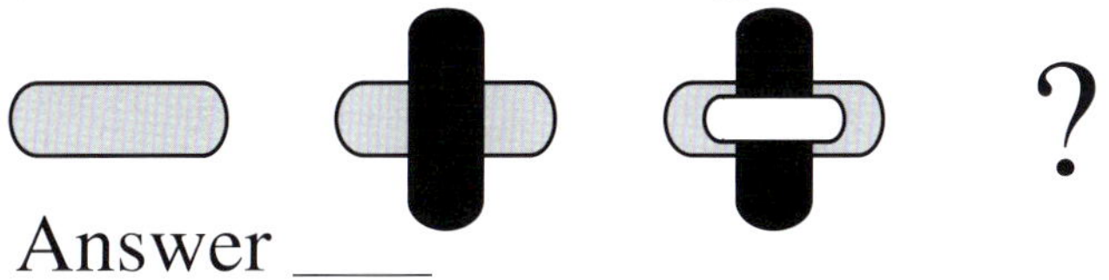

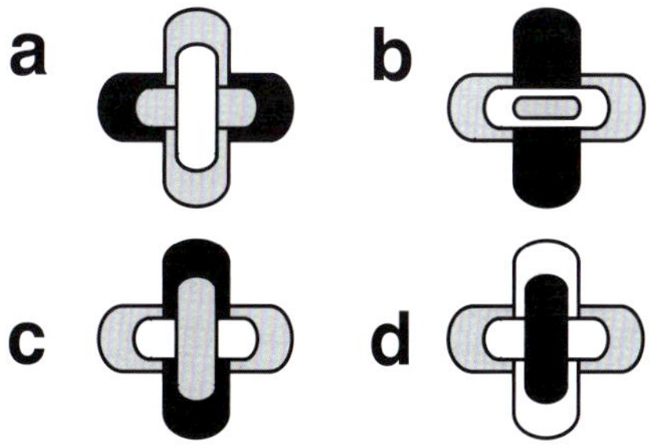

a   b   c   d

Answer _____
The correct order of block fills is:
_____ _____ _____ _____ _____

10) Which pair of figures belongs to this family of figures?

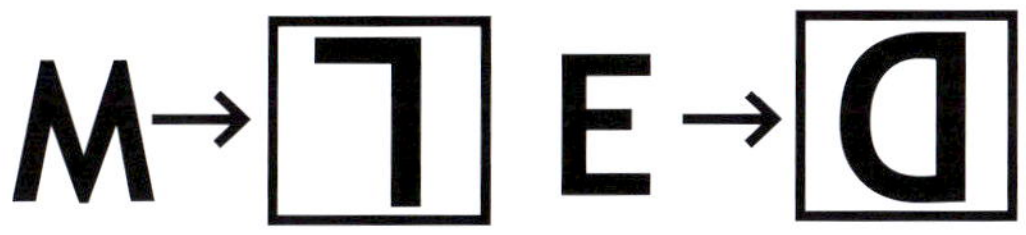

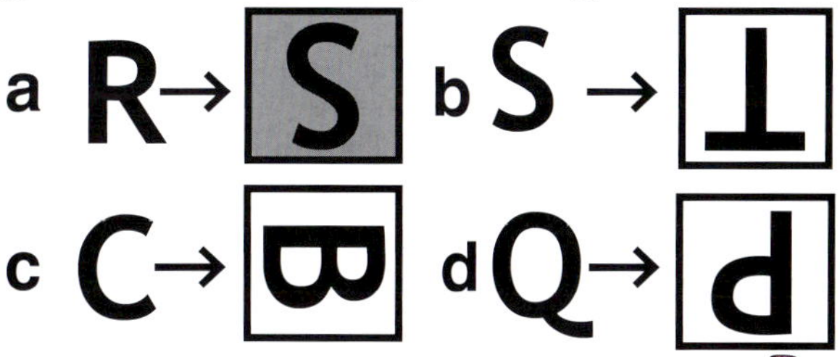

M→ □ E→ □   a R→ S   b S→ T
                c C→ B   d Q→ d

Answer _____
The three rules are:
i) _____
ii) _____
iii) _____

Score _____

3. Subtraction

In Non-verbal Reasoning, smaller shapes or parts of a shape can be **Subtracted** from the original shape or shapes.

1. Subtracting parts of shapes

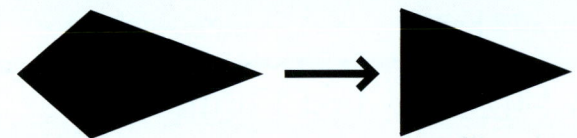

The original Kite with a Block Black Fill has had a Triangular section subtracted from it. The shape that remains is an Isosceles Triangle with a Black Block Fill.

2. Subtracting shapes

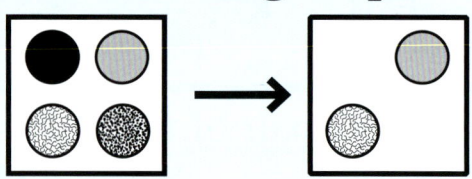

The Circles with a Speckled Fill and a Black Block Fill have been subtracted from the original group. This can also be also be understood as a change in Frequency (see pages 41-43).

Key Non-verbal Reasoning questions apply to subtractions:

Example 1: Which shape is a subtraction of the Test Shape?

 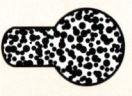   

Test Shape   a   b   ⓒ   d

Answer: **c** - It has a subtraction or missing piece.

Example 2: Which shape is not a subtraction of the Test Shape?

Test Shape   a   b   c   ⓓ

Answer: **d** - This shape has been rotated but it is the same.

Example 3: Which figure is next in the series?

    ?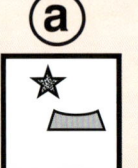

ⓐ b

c d

Answer: **a**

It is a 90° Anticlockwise rotation. The Ribbon Shape with a Black Block Fill is subtracted as it moves to the bottom left of the square.

Exercise 3: 3   Answer the following:

1) Which is the next figure in the series?

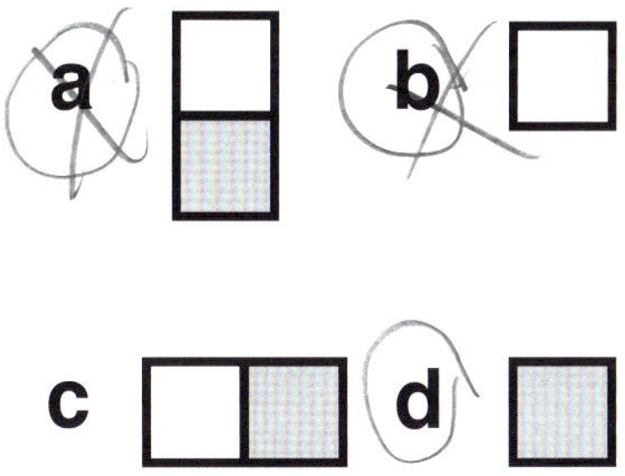

Answer __d__
A __square__ must be subtracted each time in a(n) __anti-clockwise__ direction around the shape.

2) Which pair of figures does not fit in with the others?

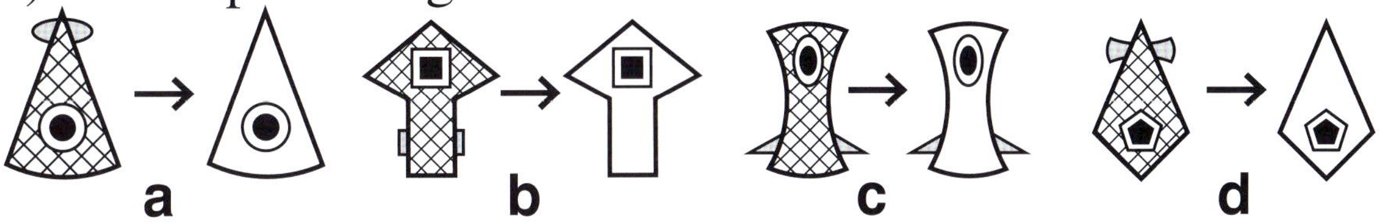

Answer __c__   What two things must be subtracted each time?
i) _____   ii) _____

3) Which figure is next in the series?

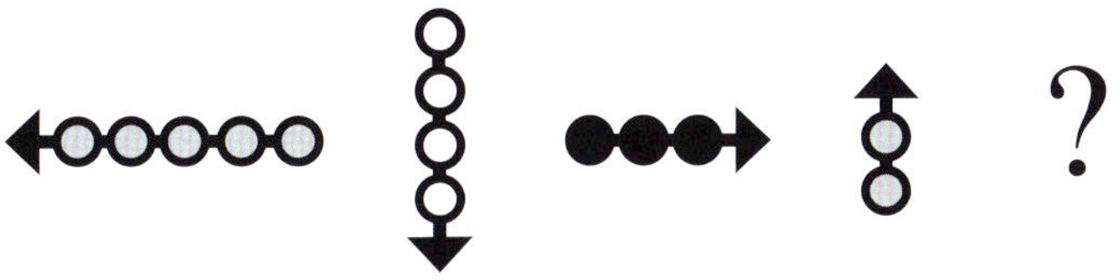

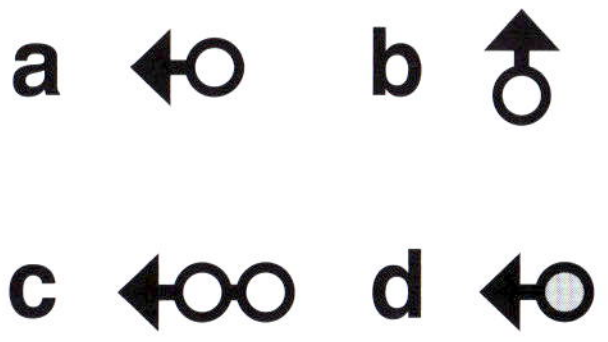

What must be subtracted each time?
Answer ____   _____

4) Which pair of figures does not fit in with the others?

Why not? _____
Answer ____   _____

5) Which is the next figure in the series?

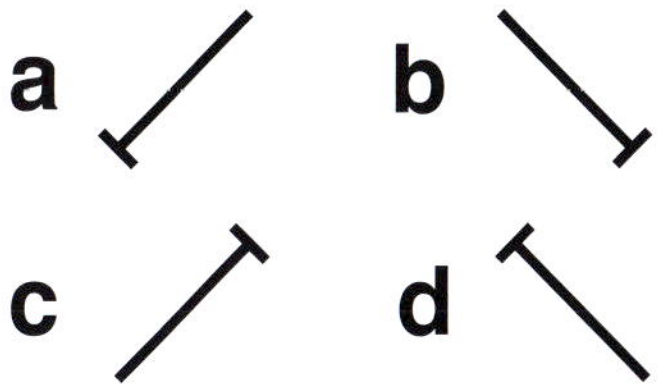

Answer ____
What is the order of subtraction? (Underline the correct answer.)
Right Slant Bar then Left Slant Bar **or** Left Slant Bar then Right Slant Bar.

6) Which two pairs of shapes are most alike?

a   b   c   d

Answer ____ and ____

What must be subtracted? _____

7) Which pair of figures is the odd one out?

a   b   c   d

Answer ____   What must be subtracted each time?
_____

8) Which pair of figures is most like the Test Figures?

Test Figures   a   b   c

Which two things must be subtracted? i) _____
Answer ____ _____ ii) _____

9) Which figure is next in the series?

?   a   b
    c   d

Answer ____

What must be subtracted? _____

10) Which pair of figures is most like the Test Figures?

Test Figures   a   b   c

Answer ____

What must be subtracted? _____

Score

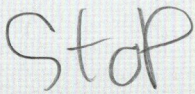

4. Frequency (Counting)

In Non-verbal Reasoning, **Frequency** involves the counting of shapes, smaller shapes within other shapes, or parts of shapes.

1. Counting shapes

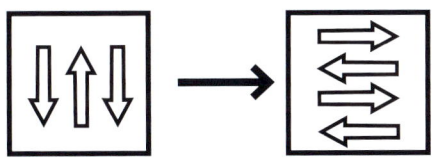

The original figure has three Vertical Arrows. The frequency (number) in the second figure is increased to four Horizontal Arrows. **This change could also be understood as an addition.**

2. Counting parts of shapes

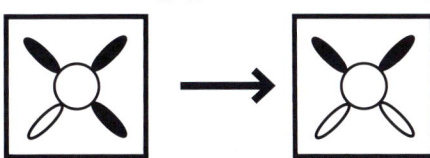

The original figure has three Ellipses with a Black Fill. The frequency (number) in the second figure is decreased to two Ellipses with a Black Fill. **This change could also be understood as a subtraction.**

Key Non-verbal Reasoning questions apply to frequency:

Example 1: Which figure is most similar to the Test Figure?

 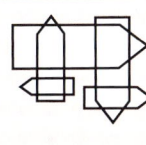  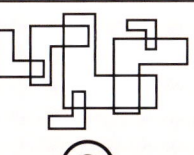 

Test Figure   a   b   c   d

Answer: **c** - It has a frequency of six like the Test Figure.

Example 2: Which figure is most different from the others?

   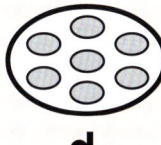 

a   b   c   d   e

Answer: **e** - It has a frequency of six rather than seven.

Example 3: Which figure is next in the series?

a   b

c   d

Answer: **b**

The frequency (number) of Squares should be eight. The fill types of the Squares are not relevant. The Equilateral Triangle should point upwards and have Vertical Shading.

Exercise 3: 4   Answer the following:

1) Which is the next figure in the series?

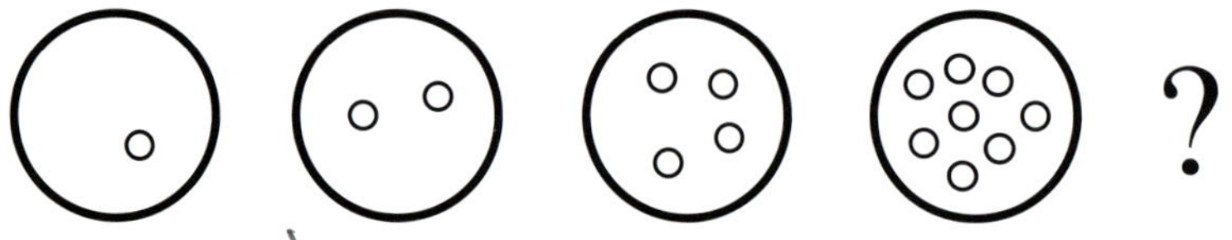

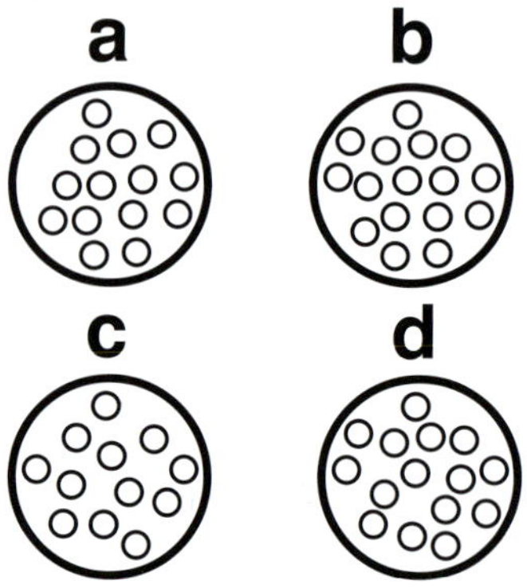

Answer b

Write out the number sequence of the five figures.
It begins with **1**, 2 4 8 16

2) Which figure does not fit in with the others?

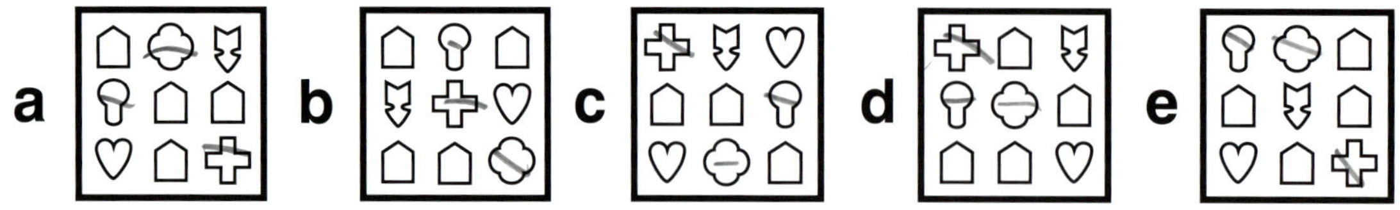

Answer ____   Why not? _____

3) Which figure belongs to this family of figures?

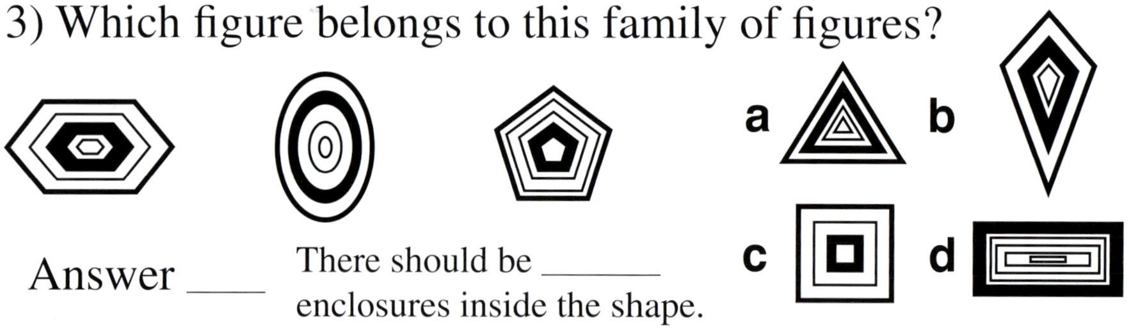

Answer ____   There should be ____ enclosures inside the shape.

4) Which pair of figures is most like the Test Figures?

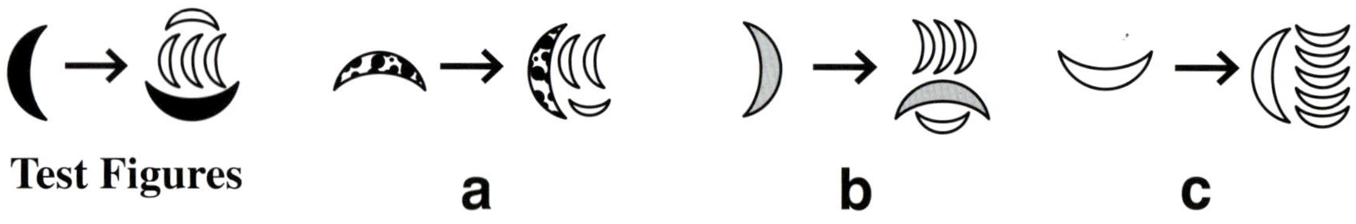

Test Figures   a   b   c

Answer ____   How many Crescent Shapes should there be? ____

5) Which pair of figures is the odd one out?

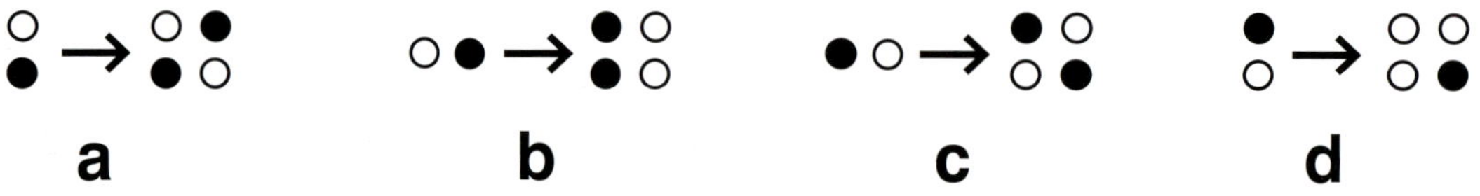

a   b   c   d

Why? _____
Answer ____

6) Which figure does not fit in with the other figures?

a   b   c   d

Why not? _____

Answer ____ _____

7) Which figure belongs to this family of figures?

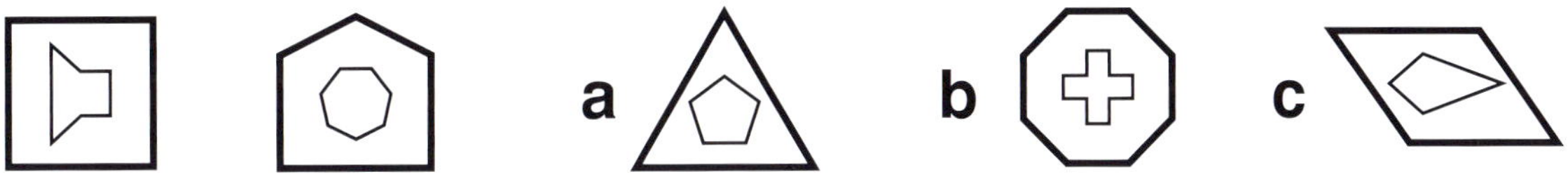

a   b   c

Answer ____   The enclosed shape should have ____ more sides.

8) Which figure does not fit in with the others?

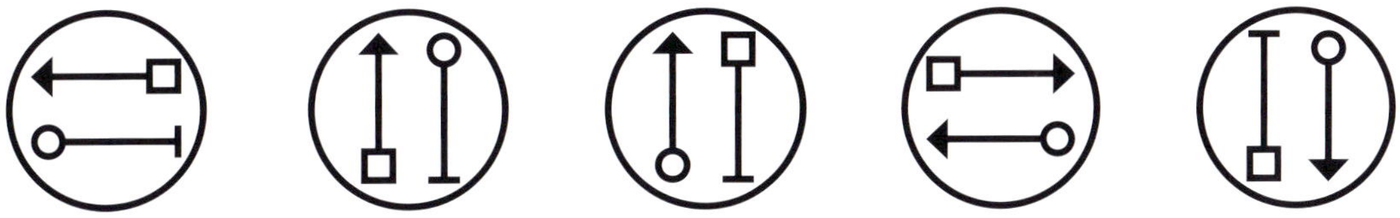

a   b   c   d   e

Answer ____   There should be ____ of each type of line ending.

9) Which is the next figure in the series?

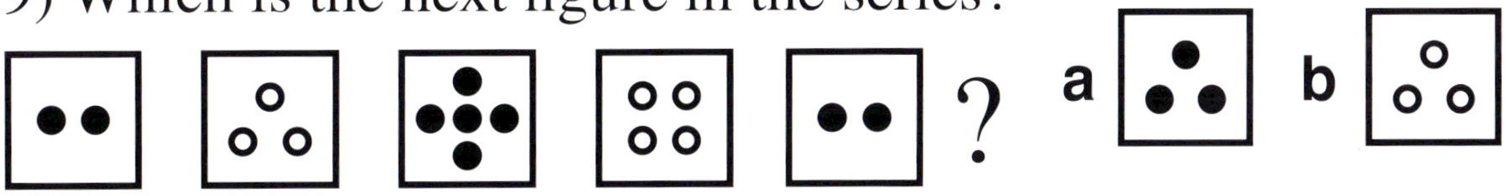

? a b c d

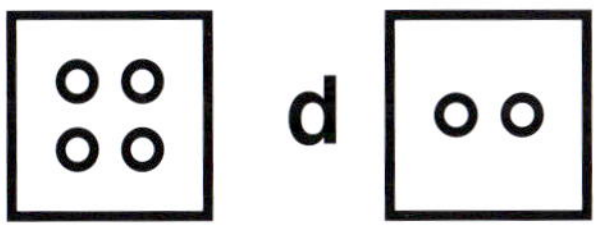

Answer ____
Write out the number sequence of the six figures.
It begins with **2**, _____

10) Which figure belongs to this family of figures?

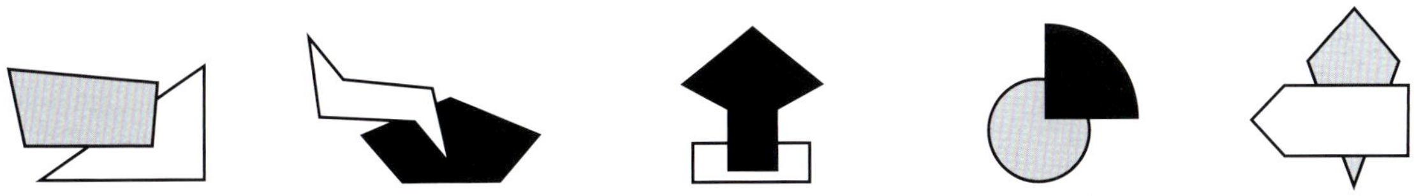

a   b   c

Answer ____   Why? _____
_____

Score ____

Chapter Four
PATTERNS

In Non-verbal Reasoning, shapes can make **Patterns** in two ways:
Repetition • Cumulation

1. Repetitive

Shapes can be be arranged in a **Repetitive** pattern:

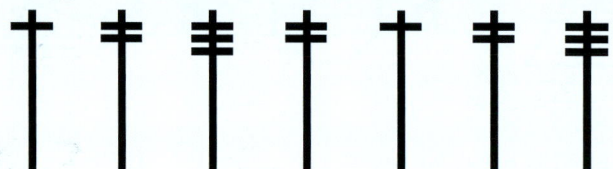

The Telegraph Poles are in a repetitive pattern of one, two, three, two, one, two, three crossbars, etc.

Key Non-verbal Reasoning questions apply to repetition:

Example 1: Which shape is first in the series?

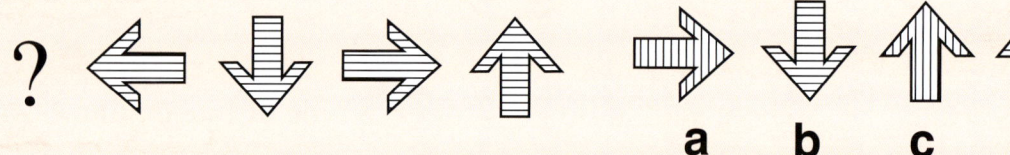

Answer: **d** - It has the correct shading and rotation.

Example 2: Which shape is missing in the series?

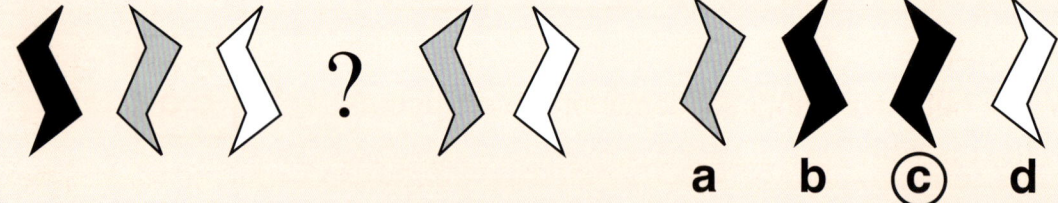

Answer: **c** - It has a Black Fill and is the correct reflection.

Example 3: Which figure is next in the series?

Answer: **c** - Both shapes have the correct fill and rotation.

Exercise 4: 1   Answer the following:

1) Which is the next figure in the series?

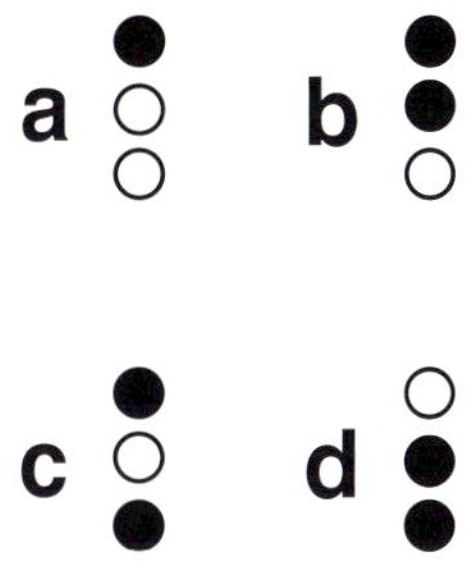

Answer ____

Write out the repetitive pattern of the Circles with a Black Fill in numerical terms. It begins with **1**, _____

2) Which figure is first in the series?

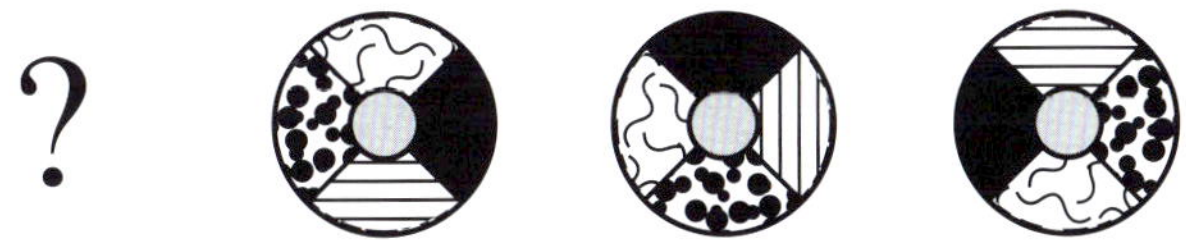

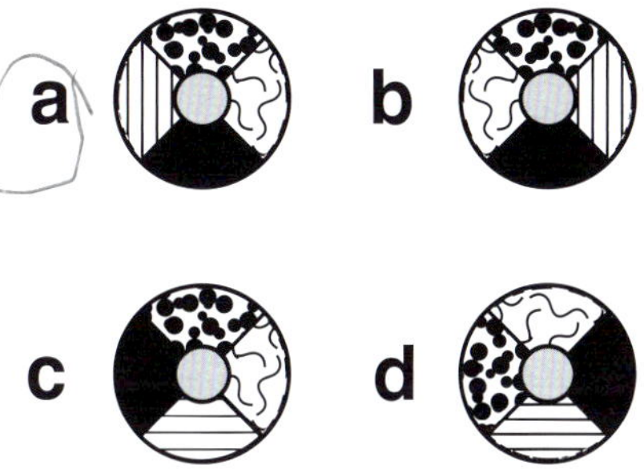

Answer ____   Do the Shaded Fills rotate Clockwise or Anticlockwise? _____

3) Which is the missing figure in the series?

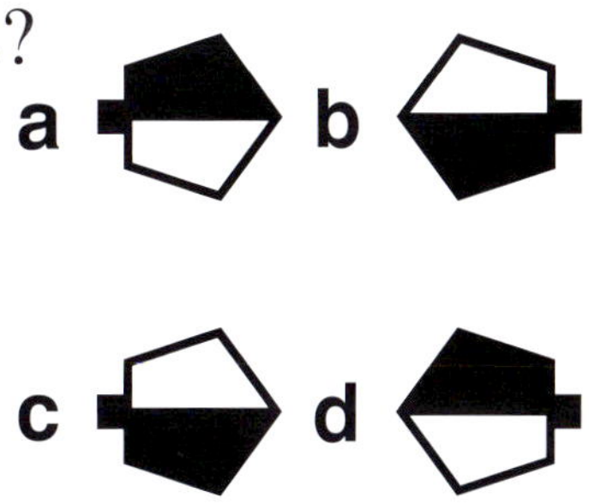

Answer ____   As the shapes are rotated, what kind of movement takes place? _____

4) Which is the next figure in the series?

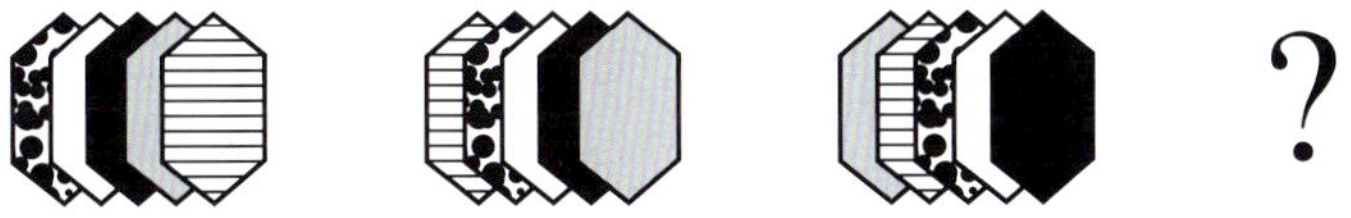

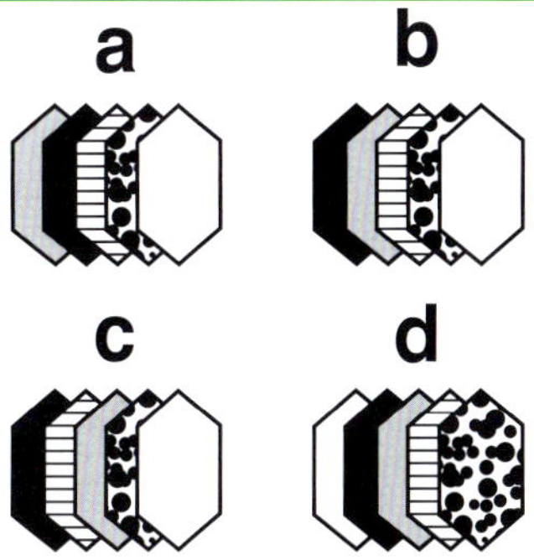

Answer ____   Write the order of Hexagon fills (front to back) of this figure. _____

5) Which figure is first in the series?

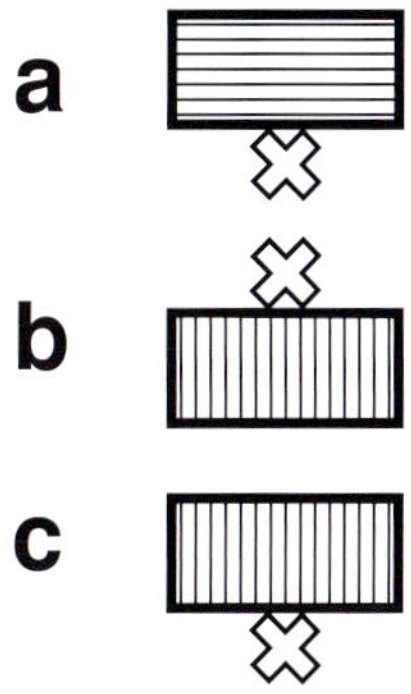

Answer ____

Describe the fill of the Rectangle in this figure. _____

6) Which is the missing figure in the series?

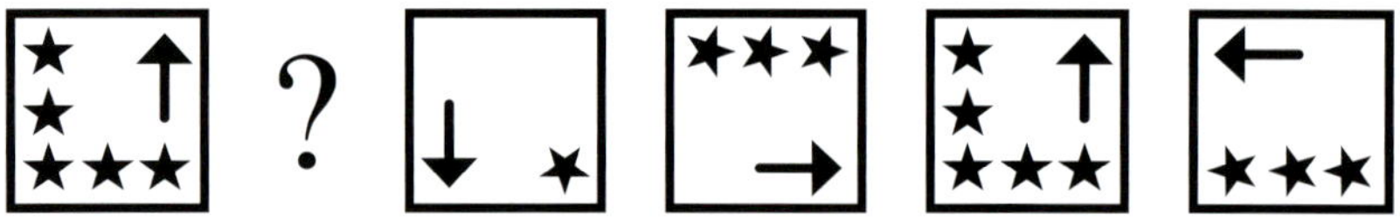

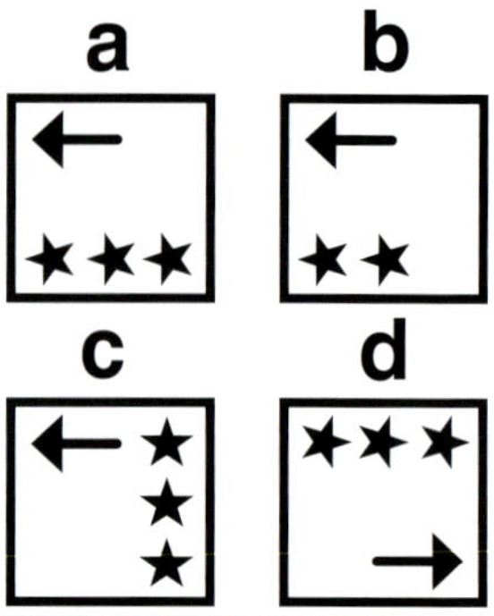

Answer ____ Write out the repetitive pattern of the Stars in numerical terms. It begins with **5**, _____

7) Which figure is next in the series?

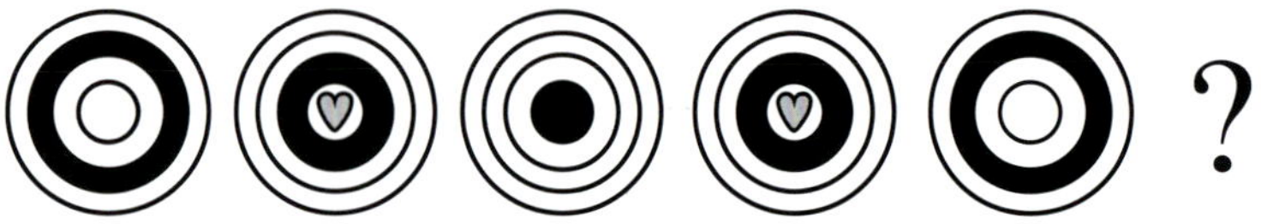

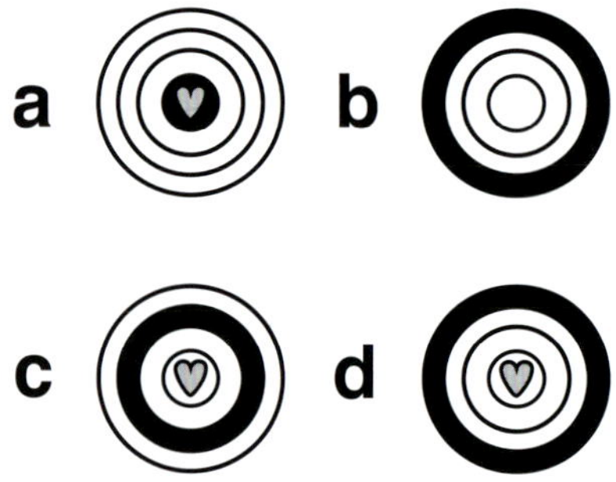

Answer ____ Which shape is repeated in every other figure of the series? _____

8) Which figure is next in the series?

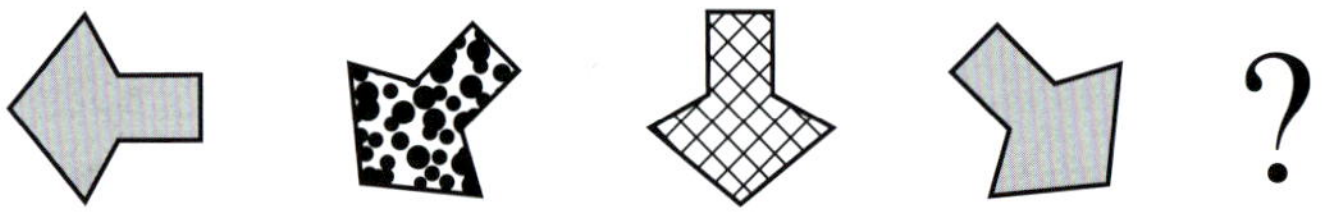

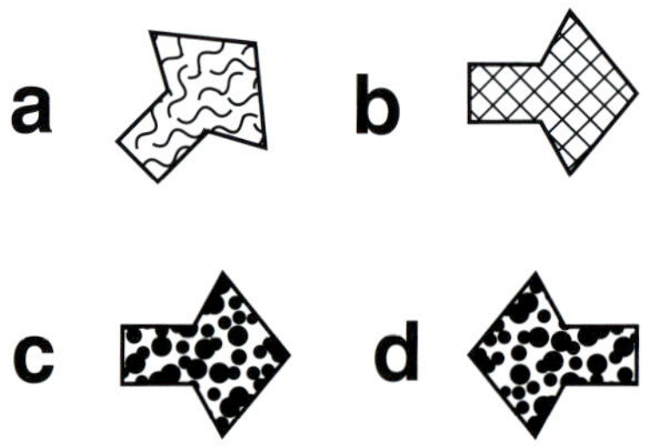

Answer ____ Write out the order of fills.
_____

9) Which figure is missing in the series?

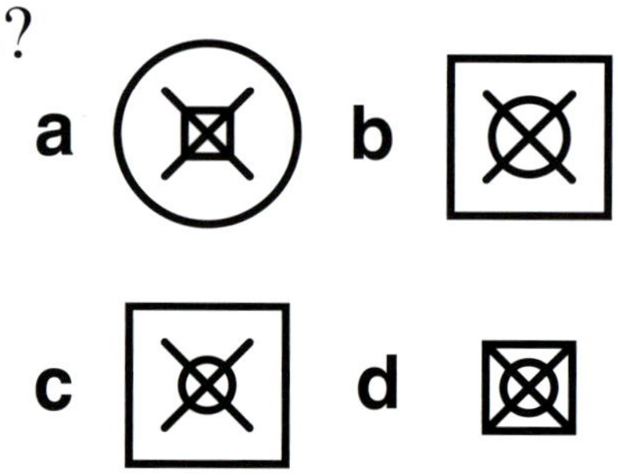

Answer ____ Describe the three-fold size progression for the Square: _____ _____ _____

10) Which is the next figure in the series?

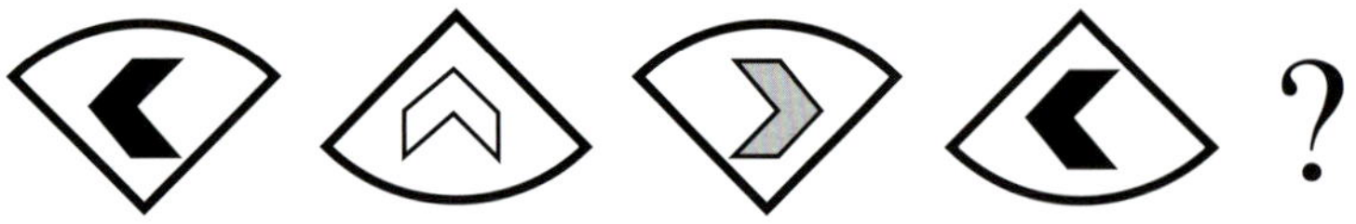

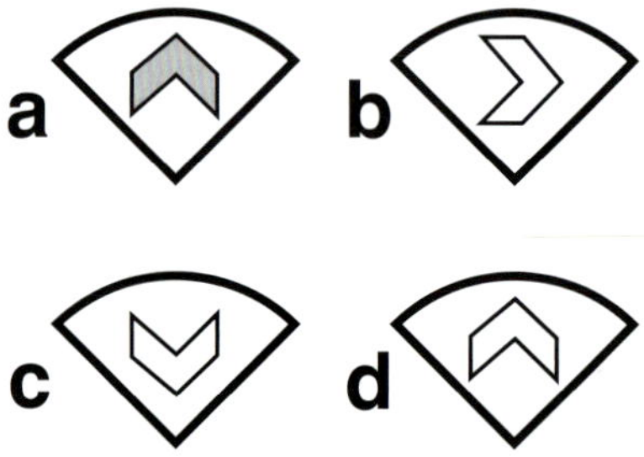

Answer ____
Study the Chevron Shape.
It rotates ____° in a(n) _____ direction.

Score ____

2. Cumulation

Shapes can be be arranged in a **Cumulative** pattern:

The Pentagon builds side by side in five stages.

Key Non-verbal Reasoning questions apply to cumulation:

Example 1: Which shape is first in the series?

 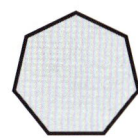    a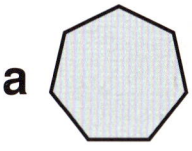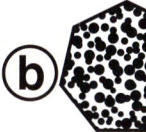

Answer: **b** is a larger shape and has the correct Liquid Fill.

c 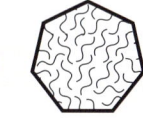 d

Example 2: Which figure is missing in the series?

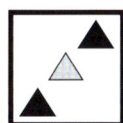   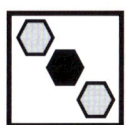 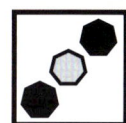   a 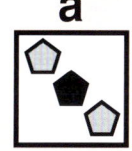 b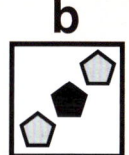

Answer: **d** has Pentagons that lie diagonally from bottom left to top right and has a fill order of Black, Grey, Black.

c 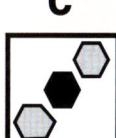 d

Example 3: Which figure is next in the series?

  ? 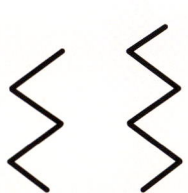 a  b 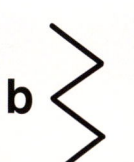 c  d

Answer: **a** has six lines so it is the correct Zigzag Line Shape. It is also the correct direction of the Zigzag Line Shape.

Exercise 4: 2   Answer the following:

1) Which is the next figure in the series?

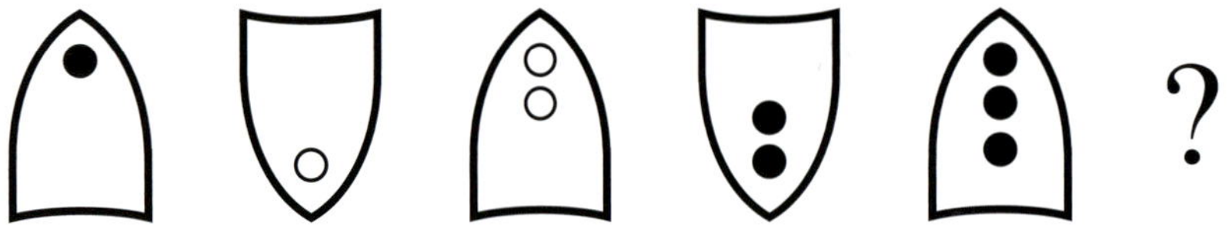

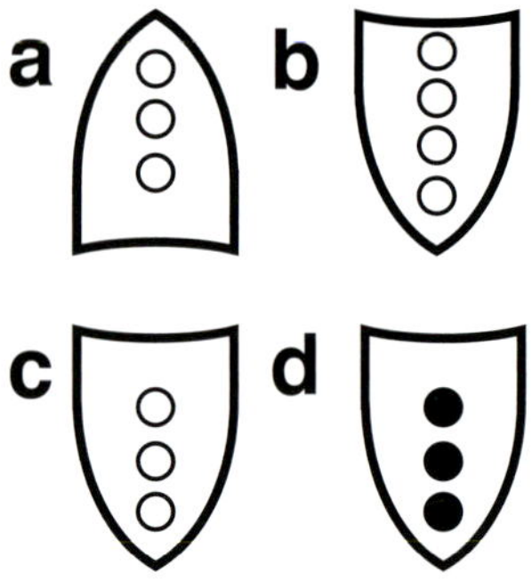

Answer __C__   Why? _____

2) Which figure is first in the series?

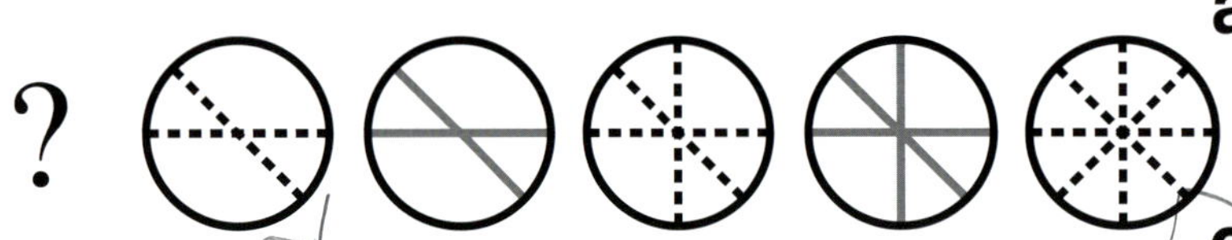

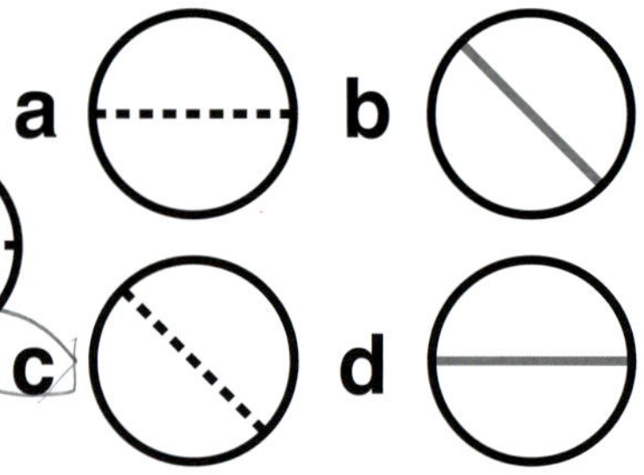

Answer __d__   Name the two types of line used:

i) _____ _____   ii) _____ _____

3) Which is the missing figure in the series?

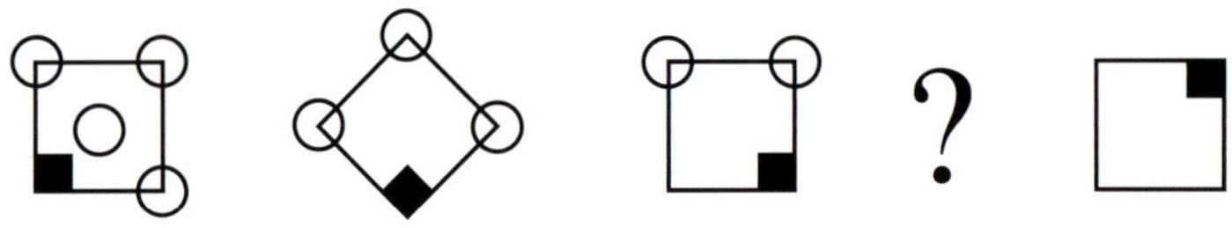

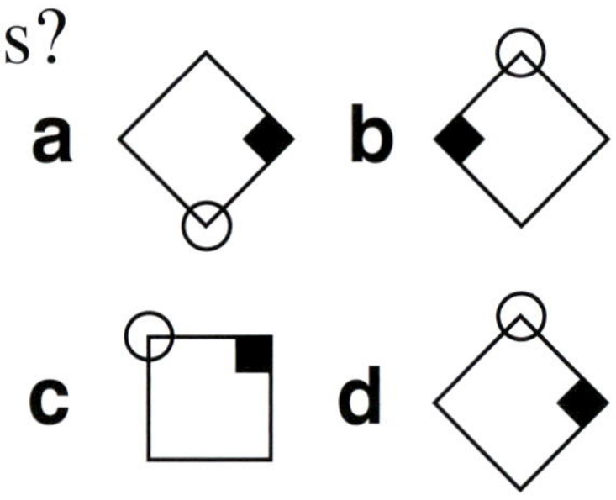

Answer ____
What shape must be subtracted each time? _____

4) Which is the next figure in the series?

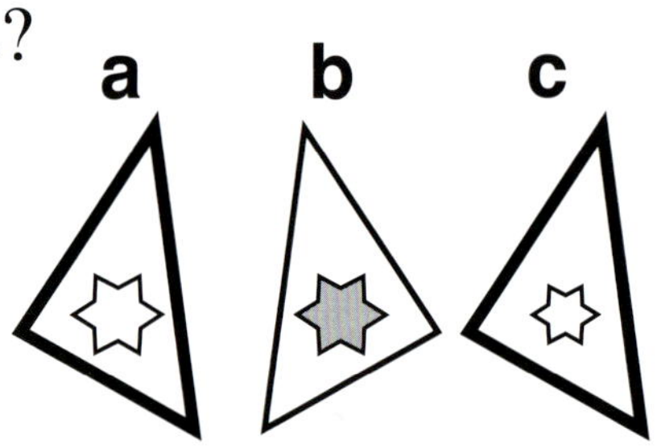

Answer ____   Which shape is cumulative? _____

5) Which figure is first in the series?

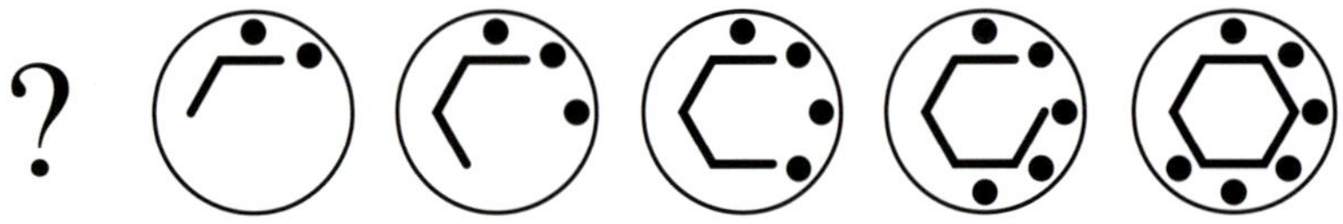

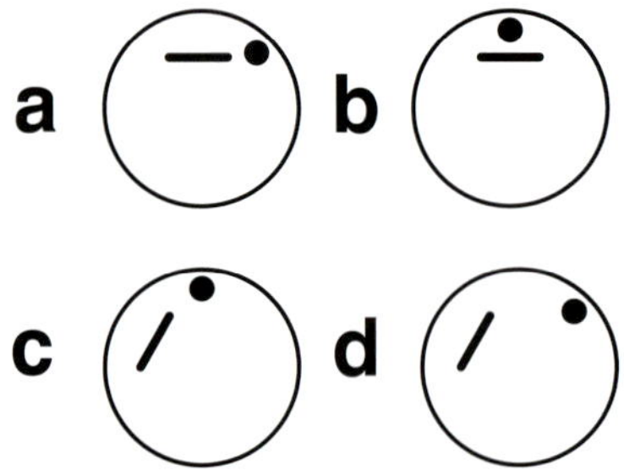

Answer ____   What two things must be added

each time? _____ and _____

6) Which is the missing figure in the series?

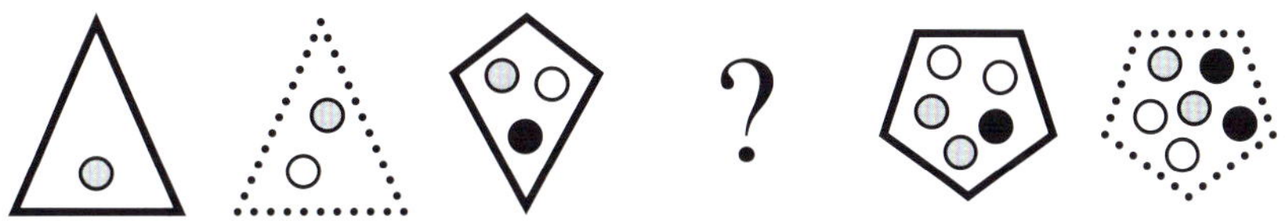

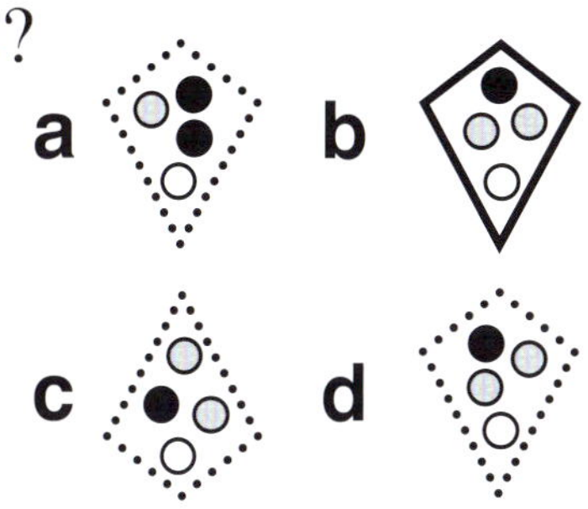

Answer ____   What shape is added? _____

7) Which is the next figure in the series?

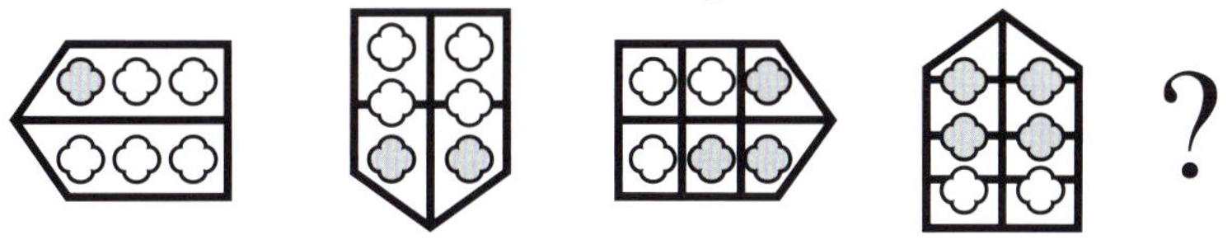

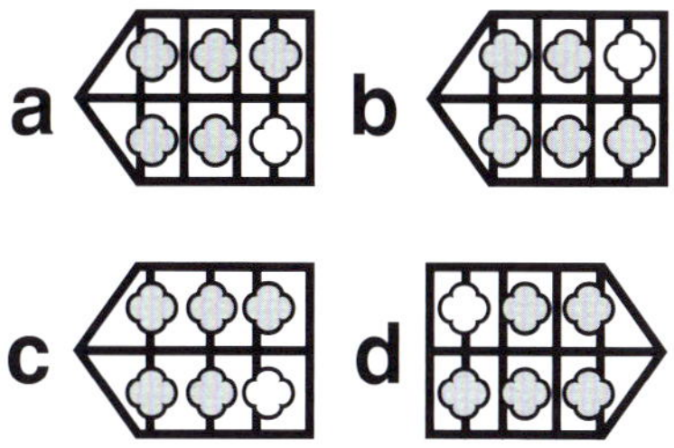

Answer ____   Name the two cumulative actions.
i) _____
ii) _____

8) Which figure is first in the series?

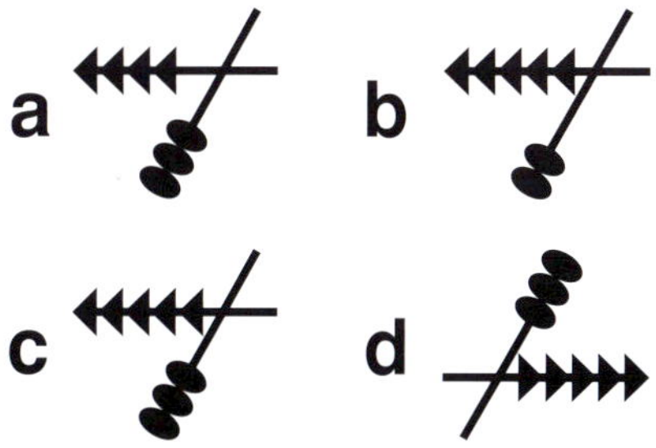

What must be subtracted?

Answer ____   _____

9) Which is the missing figure in the series?

Answer ____   Where is the Heart Shape subtracted from (front or back)? _____

10) Which is the next figure in the series?

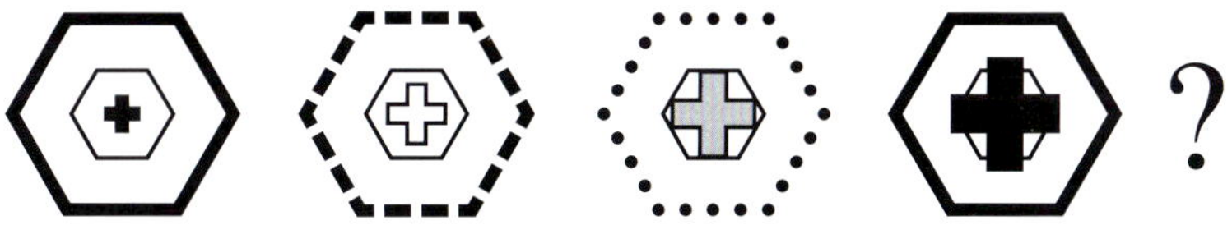

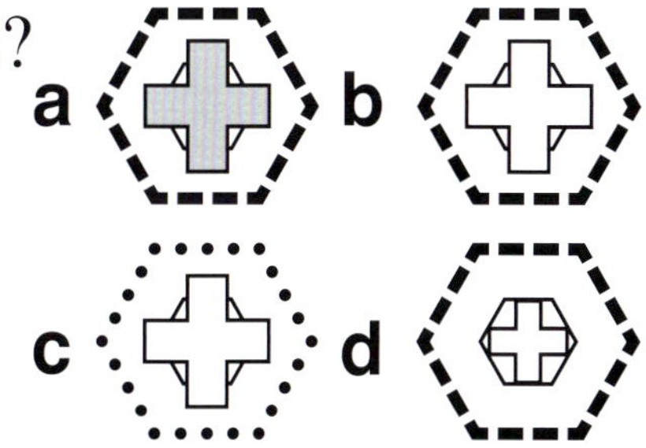

Answer ____

Write the repetitive pattern of the lines sequence of the outer Hexagon. _____

What is the cumulative action? _____

Score ☐

Chapter Five
LAYERING

Non-verbal Reasoning questions are complicated by the process of **Layering**. Questions can have up to five layers (or changes) that have to be observed to find a solution.

1. Level One

Some shapes only have one layer or change.

Test Shape

The Segment Shape has received only one layer or change. It has been rotated 180°.

Key Non-verbal Reasoning questions apply to layering:

Example 1: Which shape is most similar to the Test Shape?

  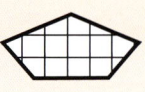 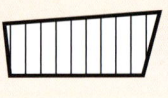 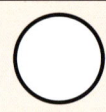

Test Shape   a   b   c   ⓓ

Answer: **d** is circular, as is the Test Shape.

Example 2: Which shape is most unlike the Test Shape?

Test Shape   a   b   ⓒ   d

Answer: **c** has a Black Fill; the Test Shape has a Speckled Fill.

Example 3: Which shape is next in the series?

     ?   a  ⓑ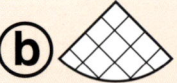

Answer: **b** has been rotated 45° in an Anticlockwise direction.

c    d

Exercise 5: 1 Answer the following:

1) Which is the next shape in the series?

Answer ____

2) Which shape does not fit in with the others?

Answer ____

3) Which figure belongs to this family of figures?

Answer ____

4) Which figure is most like the Test Figure?

Test Figure

Answer ____

5) Which shape is the odd one out?

Answer ____

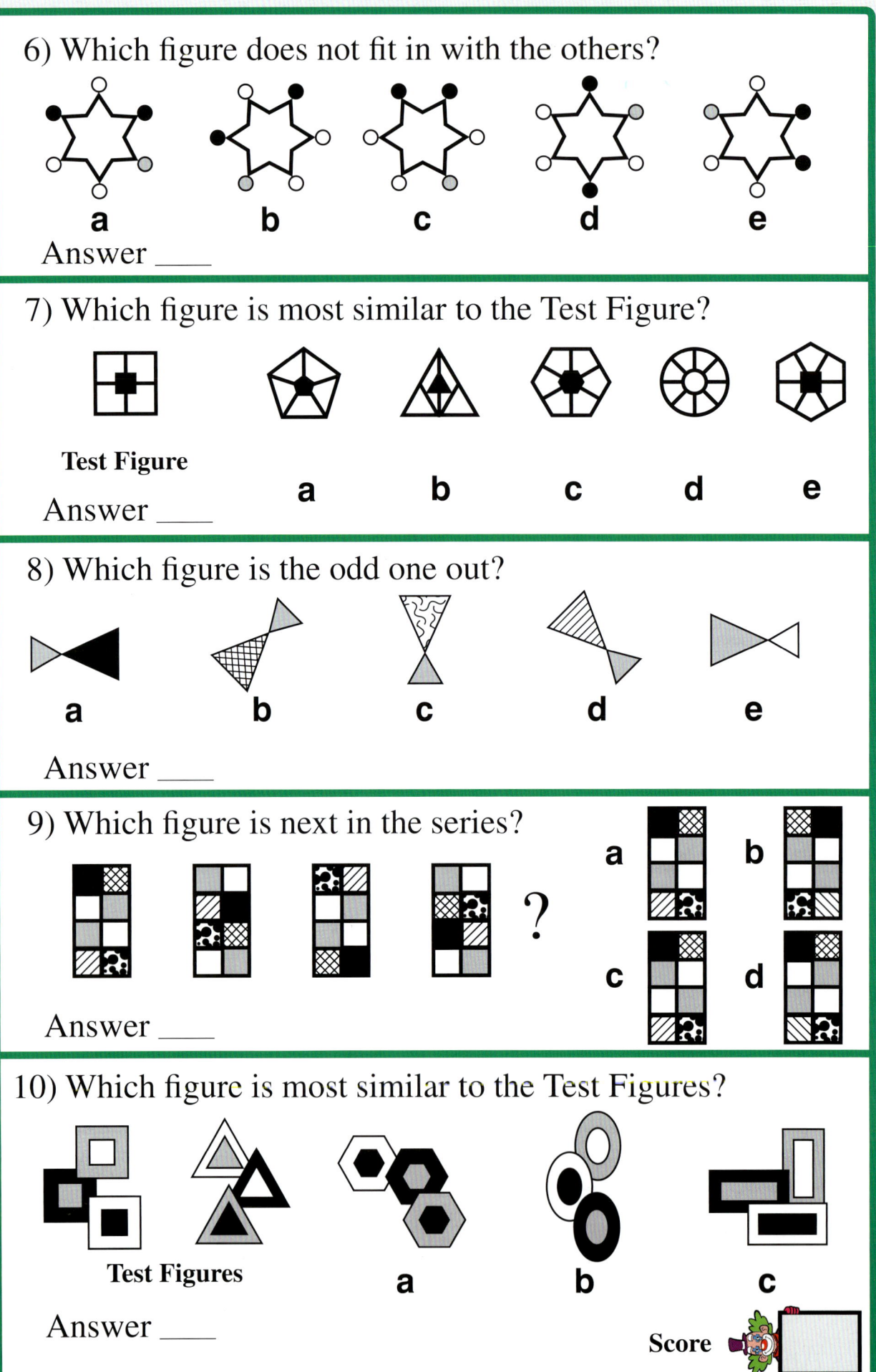

2. Level Two

In Non-verbal Reasoning, questions can have two layers:

Test Shape **Layer 1** **Layer 2**

The Pencil Shape has two layers (undergoes two changes):
Layer 1 - It has been reflected or rotated 180°.
Layer 2 - The Black Block Fill becomes a Grey Block Fill.

Example 1: Which shape completes the second pair of shapes?

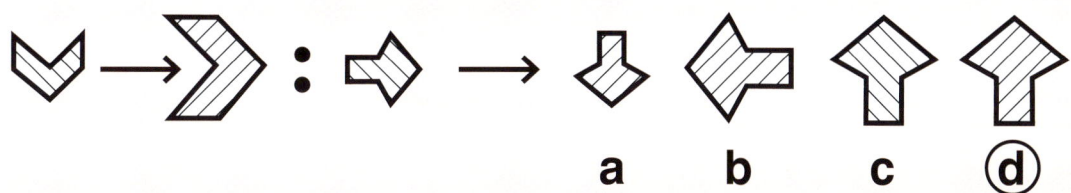

a **b** **c** **d**

Answer: **d** - The shape enlarges and rotates 90° Anticlockwise (in the same way as the first pair).

Example 2: Which pair of shapes is the odd one out?

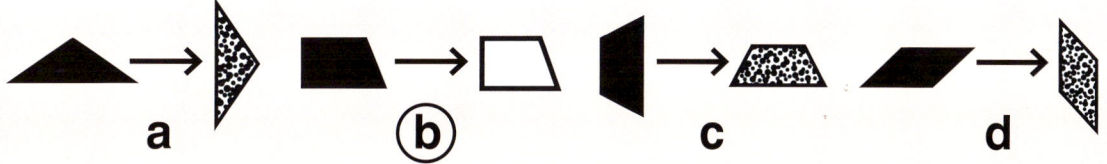

a **b** **c** **d**

Answer: **b** does not rotate and has the wrong fill.

Example 3: Which figure is next in the series?

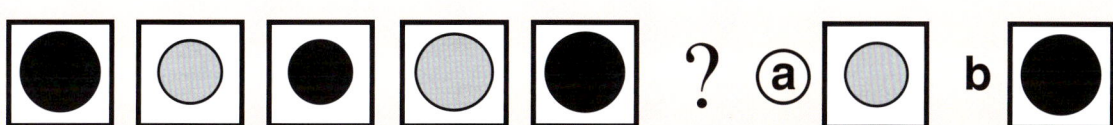

Answer: **a** has a Grey Fill (fills alternate) and it has a small Circle. (Pattern is two small Circles, then two large Circles, etc.)

Exercise 5: 2   Answer the following:

1) Which is the next figure in the series?

    a   b
    ?
    c   d

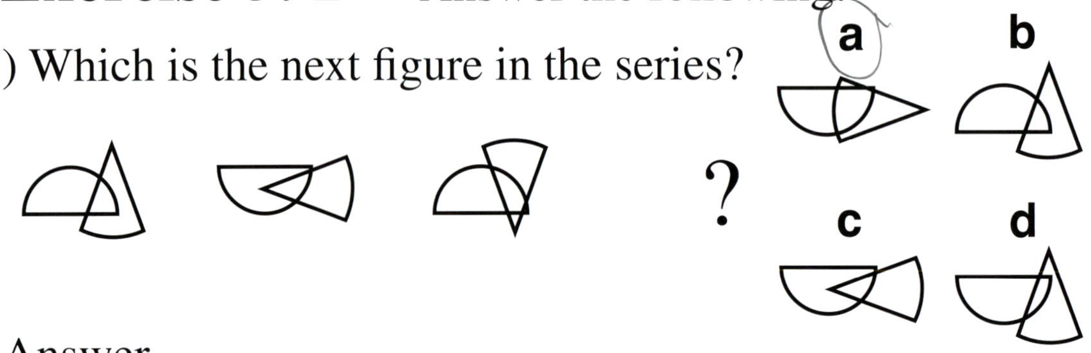

Answer ____

2) Which figure is most like the Test Figure?

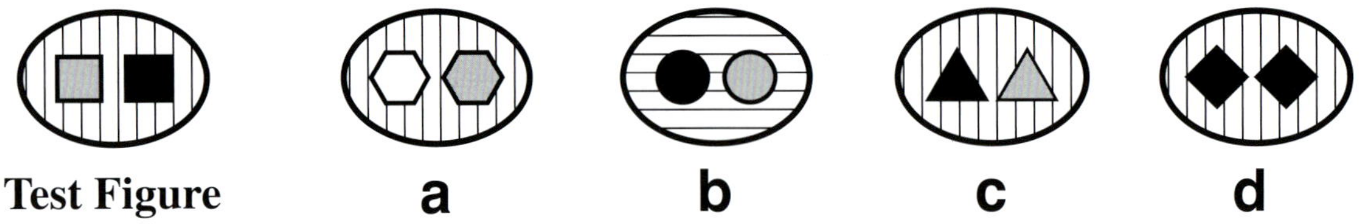

Test Figure   a   b   c   d

Answer ____

3) Which is the next figure in the series?

    a   b
    ?
    c   d

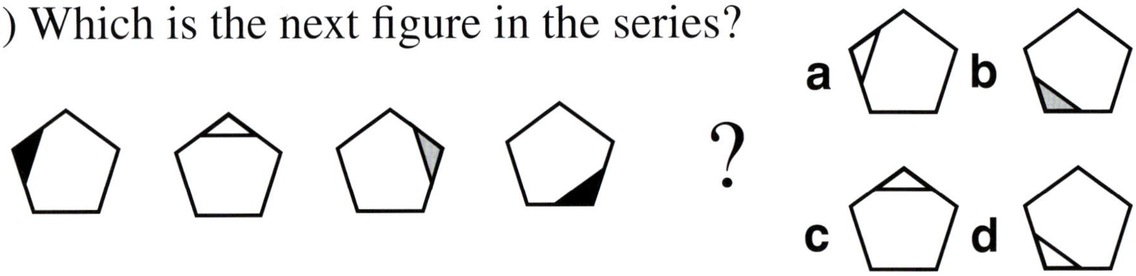

Answer ____

4) Which figure is most similar to the Test Figure?

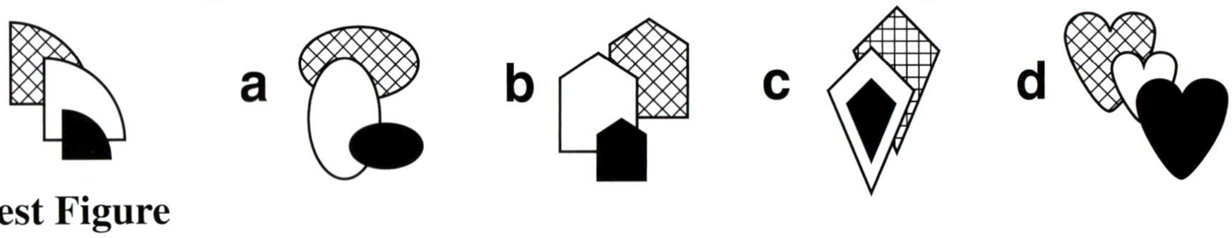

    a   b   c   d

Test Figure

Answer ____

5) Which figure is next in the series?

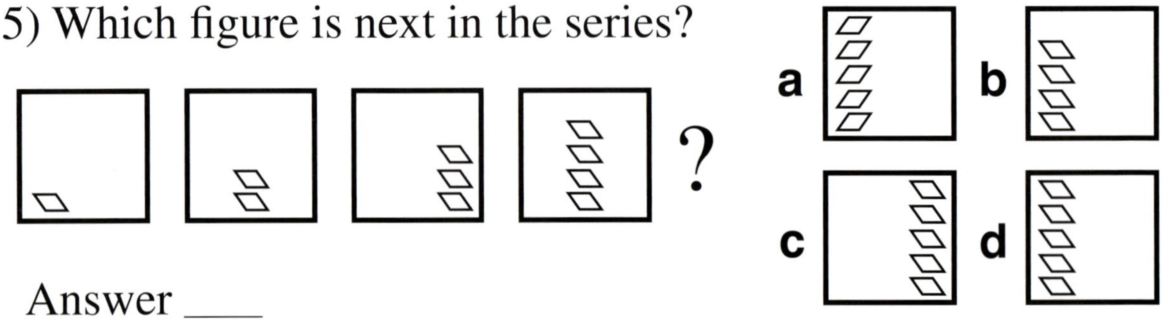

    a   b
    ?
    c   d

Answer ____

6) Which two figures are most similar?

a   b   c   d   e

Answer ____ and ____

7) Which figure is most like the Test Figure?

Test Figure   a   b   c   d

Answer ____

8) Which figure is most similar to the Test Figure?

Test Figure   a   b   c   d

Answer ____

9) Which is the next figure in the series?

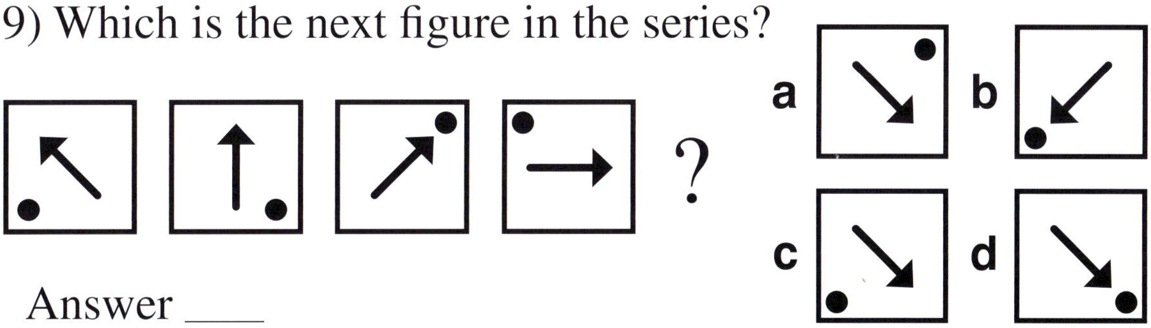

? a b c d

Answer ____

10) Which figure is most like the Test Figure?

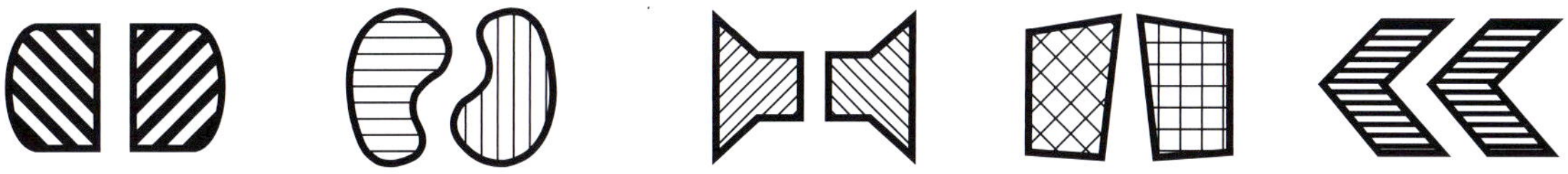

Test Figure   a   b   c   d

Answer ____

Score ____

PROGRESS CHARTS

1. ELEMENTS

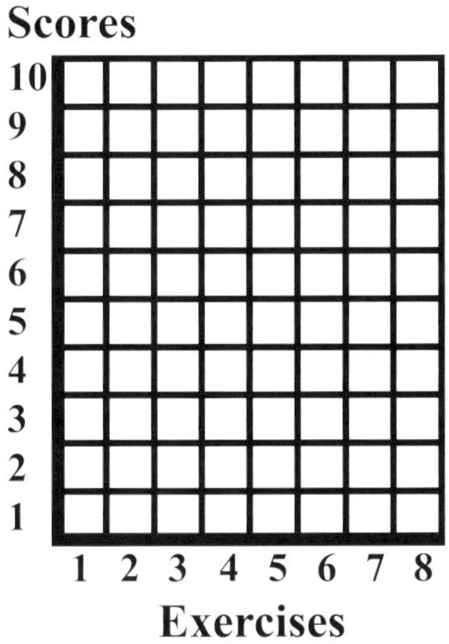

Scores — Exercises 1-8

Total Score

Percentage %

2. MOVEMENTS

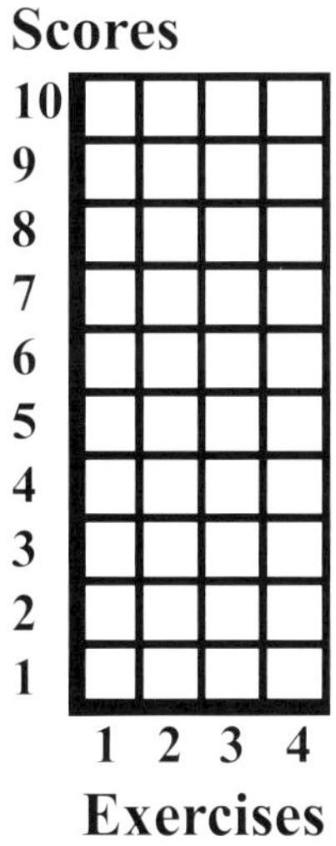

Scores — Exercises 1-4

Total Score

Percentage %

3. MANIPULATIONS

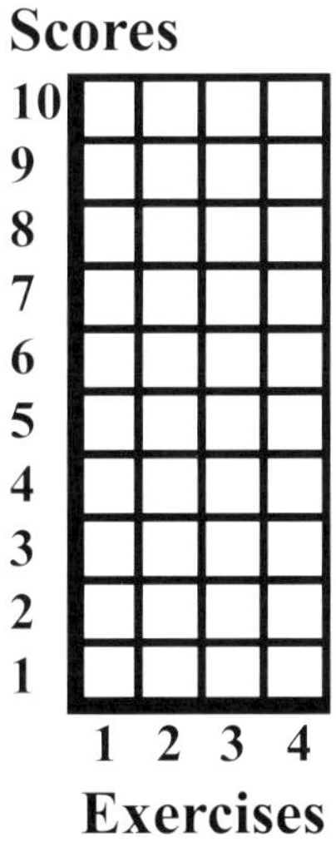

Scores — Exercises 1-4

Total Score

Percentage %

4. PATTERNS

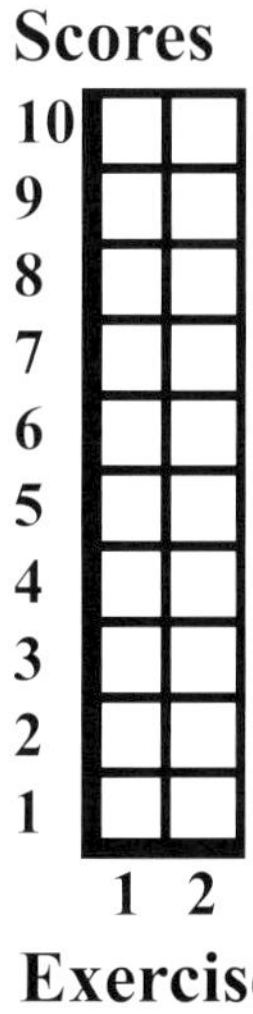

Scores — Exercises 1-2

Total Score

Percentage %

5. LAYERING

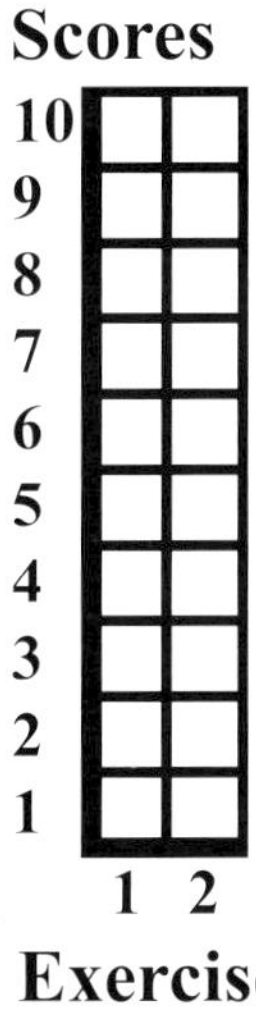

Scores — Exercises 1-2

Total Score

Percentage %

Shade in your score for each exercise on the graphs. Add up for your total score. Ask an adult to work out the percentage.

For the average add up % and divide by 5

Overall Percentage %

© 2011 Stephen Curran

CERTIFICATE OF ACHIEVEMENT

This certifies

_____

has successfully completed

11+ Non-verbal Reasoning
Year 3/4
WORKBOOK 1

Overall percentage score achieved [ ] %

Comment _____

_____

Signed _____
(teacher/parent/guardian)

Date _____